CONTENTS →

OUTFLOW

outward-focused living in a self-focused world

Steve Sjogren

Dave Ping

Dave + Pam Clark

Loveland, Colorado
www.group.com

Group resources actually work!

This Group resource helps you focus on **"The 1 Thing™"**— a life-changing relationship with Jesus Christ. "The 1 Thing" incorporates our **R.E.A.L.** approach to ministry. It reinforces a growing friendship with Jesus, encourages long-term learning, and results in life transformation, because it's:

Relational
Learner-to-learner interaction enhances learning and builds Christian friendships.

Experiential
What learners experience through discussion and action sticks with them up to 9 times longer than what they simply hear or read.

Applicable
The aim of Christian education is to equip learners to be both hearers and doers of God's Word.

Learner-based
Learners understand and retain more when the learning process takes into consideration how they learn best.

Credits

Editor: Roxanne Wieman

Creative Development Editors: Karl Leuthauser, Matt Lockhart, and Roxanne Wieman

Chief Creative Officer: Joani Schultz

Assistant Editor: Kate Nickel

Art Director: Josh Emrich

Book Designer: Jean Bruns

Print Production Artist: Joyce Douglas

Illustrator: Josh Emrich

Production Manager: Peggy Naylor

Unless otherwise indicated, all Scripture quotations are taken from the *Holy Bible,* New Living Translation, copyright © 1996, 2004. Used by permission of Tyndale House Publishers, Inc., Carol Stream, Illinois 60188. All rights reserved.

Library of Congress Cataloging-in-Publication Data

Sjogren, Steve, 1955-
    Outflow : outward-focused living in a self-focused world / Steve Sjogren and Dave Ping.
    -- 1st American pbk. ed.
    p. cm.
ISBN-13: 978-0-7644-3404-4 (pbk. : alk. paper)
1. Witness bearing (Christianity). 2. Interpersonal relations--Religious aspects--Christianity. 3. Love--Religious aspects--Christianity. I. Ping, Dave. II. Title.
BV4520.S523 2006
248'.5--dc22   2006028633

10 9 8 7 6 5 4 3 2 1   15 14 13 12 11 10 09 08 07 06

Printed in the United States of America.

DEDICATIONS

STEVE:

To Lonnie Frisbee. Though many have tried, no man-made program could ever replicate what he accomplished naturally in the power of the Spirit. May authentic love flow through us all as we become the kind of includers and inviters Lonnie was during his short life.

DAVE:

To Daphne, Ruben, and everyone who knows *there has to be more to life*. May your joy overflow beyond anything you could ever ask or imagine.

ACKNOWLEDGMENTS

Ideas don't turn into books or DVDs without lots of help from lots of different hands. We thank God for everything, but especially for our wives, Janie Sjogren and Pam Ping, who have loved, inspired, and guided us in more ways than we could ever enumerate. Somehow they've brought out the good in us in spite of the magnitude of our multiple and manifold weirdnesses.

We also thank our many friends at Vineyard Community Church, Equipping Ministries International, and the thousands of congregations around the world who have inspired and breathed life into the ideas we've put forward in this book. We especially thank Dave Workman, Steve Bowen, Doug Roe, Larry Chrouch, and Lynne Ruhl for living and sharing their stories of outflow with us. We also deeply appreciate everyone who has contributed ideas or stories through servantevangelism.com and serve-others.com.

We thank Roxanne Wieman and Candace McMahan along with all their cohorts at Group Publishing, as well as Karen Carter and the staff of EMI, for believing in this multifaceted project and working so hard to bring it into being. May God add all of our efforts together and multiply them into a flood of goodness that will bring many to the fountain of life!

—*Steve Sjogren and Dave Ping*

INTRODUCTION

It's not half empty.

It's not half full.

It's *overflowing*.

If what the Bible says is true (and we believe it is), then your life isn't meant to be anything like *half a glass* of water. God created you to be so perpetually full of rich experiences, rewarding relationships, and abundant blessings that you can afford to pour out huge amounts of hope, comfort, and refreshment on others—and still have more than you'll ever need!

*"The water that I shall give him will become in him
a fountain of water springing up into everlasting life."*

JOHN 4:14, DARBY

Imagine your life as a fountain—

the old-fashioned,

four-tiered

kind of fountain.

God is the source and your heart is the first level of that fountain. God is pouring his blessings into your life—filling you to the brim with his love, joy, and hope. Then the moment comes when you are so full that you can't possibly contain it anymore. Maybe it's a drip at first—a small bit of hope trickling from your life into someone else's—but it isn't long before the water is flowing freely and spilling into the next level of the fountain, and then the next, and the next. God's love unabated—overflowing from you into the lives of your family, friends, neighbors, community, and the world.

Outflow is outreach like you've never experienced it before:

natural,

everyday,

overflowing.

imagine...

You're waking up in the morning refreshed, revitalized. It's Monday, but you're excited for the day to begin. You pour some coffee as you smile to yourself.

"I'm loved," you think as you settle into a chair and begin to talk to your beloved…to God.

Outflow is about a richer relationship with God. A relationship like it was intended. Powerful. Intimate. Constant. It's about a conversation that never ceases—a conversation with a God who is constantly filling you up with his love, his power, and his blessings.

imagine...

You're hanging out at a pub with a friend, listening quietly as he tells you again about the problems he and his wife are having. You pray silently, desperately pleading that God would heal their marriage and turn both their hearts toward him.

He turns to you and for the first time asks if you think there's someone at your church who could help them. He's seen your marriage, watched your life, and appreciated your friendship. There's something different about you and he's thinking it has something to do with your God.

Outflow is about overflowing with God's love into your friends and family— the people who are closest to you and the people you desperately want to see experience the joy of Jesus' love.

imagine...

> *You're swinging open the door of your favorite coffee shop. As you step in you hear your name being called. You look up and see that one of the clerks—you remember her name is Shannon—has recognized you and is smiling as she waves. You smile and wave back, and then wait patiently as she finishes with her customers. You see another clerk open but decide to wait so you can talk to Shannon. As she gets your coffee, you ask about her family and her studies at the local college. She tells you things are going better than they were at the beginning of the year and she thanks you again for recommending the young adult church on campus—she's made a lot of friends there. Then she smiles and tells you that she's seriously considering this whole "Jesus thing."*

Outflow is about overflowing into your community. It's about reaching out with God's love to everyone around you. It's about natural and relational ways of engaging with the people of your city. It's about serving them with no strings attached. It's about loving them with God's love.

imagine...

> *You're on your deathbed and there are people milling all around you. You smile as you recognize so many of the faces—old faces, young faces—faces that are dear to you. As you lie there, you hear snippets of what they're saying...*
>
> *"...the world will never be the same..."*
>
> *"...touched so many lives..."*
>
> *"...good and faithful servant..."*
>
> *"...loved God so much..."*

Outflow is about a living legacy—a legacy that will last long after you're gone. It's about reaching your world—the world God has placed you in. It's about being known for loving God...and loving God's people.

Your life is meant to overflow with unimaginable joy and power.

Outflow is your field guide for discovering the truth of this God-given promise. In the next five weeks, you'll explore...

>> **How God's love can overflow through you**

>> **How you can have a richer, more meaningful relationship with God**

>> **How you can share God's love with your family and friends**

>> **How you can overflow with God's love into your community**

>> **How you can change your world through the power of God's love**

one *reading a day*

This book is designed so you can tap into what God has for you by reading and reflecting on one brief reading every weekday for the next five weeks. Of course, you could go through it much faster if you wanted to, but taking it in smaller sips, one day at a time, will allow the ideas to percolate through your mind...and begin to flow out into your life.

getting your feet wet

Faith separated from practical experience always remains in the realm of doubt. So each day we'll also provide you with an opportunity to get your feet wet through reflective activities and hands-on experiences that focus on the day's reading.

the reflection *pool*

Taking time to reflect, deliberate, and bring something into the personal context is how people grow and keep from becoming stagnant. At the end of each daily reading, take a few minutes to answer the questions in "The Reflection Pool."

If you're reading *Outflow* with your small group, set aside time during your small-group gathering to talk through the group discussion questions at the end of each week's readings.

diving into the **deep end**

Get out there and live it for yourself!

At the end of each week, you'll have an opportunity to dive into the deep end and really experience what you've been reading through practical, hands-on experiences. It might be walking through your community and praying for people or investing time and money in someone you normally wouldn't. Whatever it is, each experience will help you begin living just a bit more generously and outwardly. You'll be amazed at how each experience will change your perspective whether you do it by yourself, with your family, friends, or with a small group from your church. Be prepared for exciting results!

it's more fun with a **friend**

Outflow is about changing you, but it's also about changing the church. As a small group, commit to going through the five weeks of *Outflow* together. Meet together once weekly to discuss the group discussion questions at the end of each week's readings, and to dialogue about the ways your group can become more outward-focused. We've also designed a DVD specifically for use in your small-group gathering time. This DVD will guide your group through an exploration of outreach (the *Outflow* way!) and pose some provoking questions for your group along the way.

To purchase your small group kit, visit www.group.com/outflow or your local Christian bookstore.

how about **50** friends?

Change the atmosphere of your entire church! Commit to experiencing *Outflow* together as a congregation. The *Outflow* pastor kit is designed to lead your church through five worship services, outreach activities, and church experiences. Include your kids in this exciting program as well with the *Outflow* youth and children kits—each one designed for five weeks of growing deeper in relationship with God and overflowing into the people around them.

To purchase, check out www.group.com/outflow or visit your local Christian bookstore.

go...**outflow!**

In the weeks to come—through the daily readings, personal experiences, and small-group activities—you'll get to embrace God's shockingly positive promises, remove any obstacles that might be blocking their flow in your life, and experience God's love with far greater fullness than ever before. You'll also learn some simple, but world-changing ways to keep God's kindness flowing into you and through you to many, many others.

Your world will never be the same!

a life overflowing

"May the God of hope fill you
with all joy and peace
as you trust in him, so that you
may overflow with hope
by the power of the Holy Spirit."

ROMANS 15:13 (NIV)

"What are we born for?"

"For infinite happiness," said the Spirit.
"You can step out into it at any moment..."

—C.S. Lewis, *The Great Divorce*

READING 1

experiencing outflow

Splash...A tiny drop of rain fell from heaven as Theresa's dented Toyota idled roughly in the Taco Bell drive-through. A single mom, she depended on a government welfare check to feed her 8-year-old son. It was 10 days till the next check would arrive and she was already broke. Here's how she described what happened:

> After looking under the sofa cushions, all the car seats, and through the glove box, we came up with a grand total of...$4.58! It had been a hard week and my thinking was, "Hey, any way you look at it we aren't going to have enough money to make it through to the next check. So let's go out with style." So we headed for Taco Bell.
>
> As we got to the drive thru window to pay, I was never so shocked in all of my life. The guy standing in the window had a big grin on his face and said, "This is your lucky day—the people in front of you paid for your entire meal. They said to give you this card."
>
> The card read, "We hope this *small act of service* shows you God's love in a practical way," but I've got to tell you something, for me and my 8-year-old son, Donny, this was no *small* act of love. It was *huge*. We were in exactly the right place at exactly the right time to receive this touch from God when we needed it most!

The next day, Theresa and Donny came to church for the very first time. That tiny drop of generosity they'd experienced in God's name made them hopeful that perhaps God really did care about them and what they were going through.

11

A Promise From God

Maybe, like Theresa, you've wondered about God. Does God exist? Does he really care about me? Are God and religion even relevant anymore? My life is filled with technology, busyness, and modern problems—what, honestly, does an old-fashioned God have to do with my life?

Or maybe you already know God. Maybe you're asking different questions...questions like: How can I have a deeper relationship with God? How can I have a more authentic faith—one that's reflected in every part of my life? How can I trust God for my health, finances, and future? How can I share my hope in God with the people around me?

It doesn't matter where we are in our faith—on which part of the belief spectrum we're standing—we all have questions. We have deeply rooted and deeply critical questions. Questions whose answers will ultimately define the way we live.

The *Outflow* book is dedicated to exploring some of these difficult questions and God's biblical promises. Promises that answer our questions. Promises whose essential messages boil down to this:

Your life is meant to overflow with unimaginable joy and power.

As you read the sentence above, you might have been thinking, "No way! Maybe that's possible for extraordinarily holy people like Mother Teresa or Billy Graham, but not for everyday people like me!" And if these promises came from anywhere south of heaven, you would be right. They would seem completely ridiculous. But the fact is they come directly from the mouth of the Lord, and they permeate the very fabric of both the Old and New Testaments:

> "The Lord will guide you always; he will satisfy your needs in a sun-scorched land and will strengthen your frame. You will be like a well-watered garden, like a spring whose waters never fail" (ISAIAH 58:11, NIV).

> "Everyone who drinks this water will be thirsty again, but whoever drinks the water I give him will never thirst. Indeed, the water I give

him will become in him a spring of water welling up to eternal life" (JOHN 4:13-14, NIV).

If that doesn't add a little credibility, our advice is to give *Outflow* a try for the next few weeks and, as the Bible says, "Taste and see that the Lord is good" (PSALM 34:8).

Here's a story of how our friend Lynne first tasted the joy of this overflowing life we're talking about:

I met Gail many years ago at our husbands' office Christmas party. After doing the small-talk thing, we realized we were both stay-at-home moms with young children. I tried hard not to cringe visibly as Gail wearily described her life to me. She'd just moved to town recently and was housebound most of the time taking care of her three children—*all of them less than 3 years old!*

I was stressed-out just taking care of my 4-year-old. I couldn't even imagine how hard it would be to care for *three* little ones, and without the help and support of local friends or family. I was getting worn out just thinking about it.

Which might explain why I stopped thinking about it, because, to be honest, I'd completely forgotten about Gail and her struggles until a few days later.

At that point I'd just started getting serious about Jesus in my life so I was new at the whole prayer thing. But after I'd asked God to bless me and my family and a few of my friends, Gail came back to mind. So I asked God to please send her someone to give her a day off from her parenting duties. When I was finished, I was feeling pretty good about what a sensitive Christian I'd become. But God wasn't quite done yet. As I stood up and went about my business, I got the sense that God wanted me to be part of his answer to my prayer for Gail.

I needed a little prompting, but after thinking about it for a bit, I got her number and gave her a call. "Gail," I said, "You may not remember me, but we met at the Christmas party last week. Yes, I enjoyed meeting you, too. Today I'm calling because I'm convinced your heavenly Father loves you so much he wants to give you a full day off."

As you might imagine, Gail wasn't exactly sure how to respond to that. After her silence had stretched for several long seconds, I jumped in.

"I'm serious. You pick a day and I'll come over and take care of your kids from 9:00 in the morning until you're ready to come home that evening. You can go anywhere you want and do whatever you want." After another pause, Gail said it was nice of me to offer and she would think about it.

Sensing that she wasn't quite sure, I pressed on. "Just pick a day and I'll come over. And if you don't pick a day, I'm going to show up anyway." And, in the end, that's how it happened. I showed up at her house one morning. After she decided I wasn't crazy or a criminal, she gave in and agreed to let me watch her kids. That's when I told her I'd reserved a hotel room in her name if she wanted to have a nice place to take a nap—and that I wouldn't be upset if she didn't use it.

Gail left the house and didn't return again until 9:30 that evening. When she walked in the kids were all tucked in bed, her husband was watching TV, and I had dinner waiting for her. A smile on her face, Gail asked, "Why did you say you were doing this?"

Once again, I said simply, "Because your heavenly Father wants you to know he loves you!"

Something in Gail changed that day. The long hours away from her house and children caused her to recognize that she'd been suffocating emotionally, all the while never asking her husband or anyone else for help. After that day she finally had the courage to ask. And when she did ask, Gail was amazed at how willing he and others were to help lighten her load.

I thought all this was a great answer to my prayer, but God wasn't done yet. There was something even more exciting to come. A couple of weeks later, Gail called me up on the phone. "Tell me again, why did you decide to help me?" she asked.

And for the third time, I repeated, "Because your heavenly Father wants you to know he loves you!"

I could hear her quietly crying in the background for several seconds before she whispered, "I want to know him."

Gail talked to Jesus for the first time that day. She recognized she needed a savior and began a friendship with him.

Again you might think this would be a good end to the story, but no. A few months after that phone call, Gail began a ministry in her church—one specifically designed to give practical help to mothers of young children!

It's a life overflowing. A life that looks a lot like what Jesus describes:

"Whoever believes in me…streams of living water will flow from within him" (JOHN 7:38, NIV).

And, in this case, it all began with Lynne believing in God enough to release his love and let it overflow from her life to Gail's. Through Lynne's caring actions and simple words, God poured living water into the thirsty places of Gail's life until she began believing…and overflowing, too.

It's so refreshing, so *incredible* to feel God's love cascading into you and through you to others. It's like Lynne says, "I don't know how to describe it, other than to say I experienced God's *intense pleasure* at what we'd accomplished together that day and all that flowed out of it. "This," she declares, "is what I was made for. I want more!"

Jars of Clay

If you're still thinking you're unworthy or inadequate or that you don't know enough, perhaps you've never heard what the Bible says about "everyday people." Hard as it may be to believe, God fills our flawed and imperfect lives with his perfect Holy Spirit. This is best described in 2 Corinthians 4:7: "But we have this treasure in jars of clay to show that this all-surpassing power is from God and not from us" (NIV).

Did you get that? God has put *his treasure* in us—even though we are like jars of clay, inadequate and unworthy of holding such a precious thing. But God has given us this *all-surpassing power* (do you believe that God has given you that kind of power?) so that he might be glorified through us.

It's humbling, but as Lynne so aptly pointed out, *it's what we're made for.* God created us for this kind of life—this overflowing, abundant, rich life. God made each of us a vessel—a unique jar of clay—to be filled and overflowing with his love, grace, joy, and power.

It's beautiful. It's true. And it's what the rest of this book is all about.

A Lifestyle, Not a Program

Our goal in writing this book is not to simply give you one more interesting program or Bible study to inspire and entertain you. No, we want to help you discover and tap into a refreshing *new kind of life*—one in which you are constantly drinking in the fresh, invigorating water of heaven's goodness and pouring it out into the lives of everyone around you.

And along the way, you'll notice some changes. Your relationship with God will start to feel different…more natural, more fluid. And as your friendship with God changes and grows, we believe you'll also notice your relationships at home, work, in your neighborhood, and even at church becoming fresher—more powerful.

Instead of adding another self-help book to your shelves, we wanted to put a *practical field guide* into your hands. *Outflow* is a guide to personally connecting with God and loving everyone you meet into a friendship with Christ—all in refreshingly natural ways. Check it out…

First, *Outflow* is a *practical field guide*, which means it's about actually *doing* things rather than just talking about theories or telling inspiring stories. Sure, we'll do a little of that, too; but the main event is always about translating good thinking into helpful actions. And it's a field guide, which means *Outflow* should be used *out in the field*. It's filled with sensible, useful advice to help you get around better in the environment where you're living and working.

To many reading this book, *connecting with* God probably still sounds a little theoretical, while to others it's a fact of your everyday existence. No matter where you are in your faith and relationship with God, this is a book that will help you move forward. It's about relating with Jesus in some of the same ways you do with your best friends. It's about feeling his love more truly and deeply than ever—and loving Jesus in the ways that mean the most to him. It's also about sharing the riches of this wonderful relationship by loving everybody around you closer and closer to him.

When we say *loving everybody toward Christ*, we're talking about relating to people in ways that say, "You're precious to God, and he wants you to know it." We're not just talking about religious words, but thoughtful actions and focused sharing—the kind that really helps people to *see* and *feel* God's love. And when we say *everybody*, we're talking about you, your family, your husband or wife, your boyfriend or girlfriend, your sports buddies or shopping companions. We're talking about the folks you work with, go to school with, barbecue with, or sit with to watch your child's soccer game. We're also talking about your waiters, barbers, professors, garbage collectors, gardeners, receptionists, tax accountants, people you're barely acquainted with, and total absolute strangers. No one gets left out.

Finally, when we say that you can do all of this in *refreshingly natural ways*, well, that's just what we mean. It's not about dutifully struggling your way through scripted agendas or mumbling impersonal religious slogans. It's not about guilt or doing it because you're a Christian and you feel like you should. Instead, it's about truly understanding your relationship with God. It's about having an authentic friendship with God and living free of guilt and worry—living with *confidence* and *power* in God's Spirit. Once you've got that, your desire for service and outreach will flow naturally *from* your relationship with God. You'll find yourself *really* caring for everyone around you—for their present needs and their eternal ones. You'll genuinely want to connect with the essential things that make them tick. And in doing so, you'll discover a wonderful richness in your friendships and a depth of connection you probably never dreamed possible.

It sounds great, right? If not a little...idealistic. Well, we'll understand if you're still a bit skeptical at this point. After all, we've only told you about *Outflow* and how it works...you haven't experienced it for yourself yet. But just wait, once you've experienced the blessings of living an outward-focused, overflowing life you'll never be the same—and neither will the people around you!

So come on...take the plunge. We think you'll find the water to be just right.

getting your feet wet

After each daily reading, we'll provide a brief opportunity to apply some of what we just talked about in order to get your feet wet. Since this chapter is your introduction to the whole *Outflow* thing, we think it might be a good idea to begin with a prayer. And instead of providing that prayer for you, we thought maybe the best person to pray for you...is you.

If you're new to the whole "prayer thing," it's easier than you might think. It's just talking to God as honestly as possible...even if you don't fully believe in him yet. (Speaking of honesty, go ahead and tell God you're not sure if you believe yet. Far from striking you down with lightning, God will reach out to you and help you believe.) Just be honest. Seriously. No fancy words. No exact formulas. Just talk to him like you would a friend. So whether you're sitting on the beach right now, hanging out in your living room listening to music, or sipping coffee at a café, go ahead and start talking. Say "Hello, God," and then tell him what you hope to experience and learn during the next month. That's all there is to it.

Take a minute to jot down a summary of what you said to God. That way—after a month of putting *Outflow* into practice—you can come back and see how God has answered your prayer.

....

....

....

....

....

....

....

....

the reflection pool

>> What are your questions about God?

>> If those questions were answered, how might the answers change your life?

>> If you could use one word to describe your emotions after reading this chapter, what would it be? Why that word?

>> What are your hopes in reading this book?

"THE WATER THAT I SHALL
GIVE HIM WILL BECOME
IN HIM A FOUNTAIN OF
WATER, SPRINGING UP
INTO ETERNAL LIFE."

—JOHN 4:14
(DARBY)

"Talk not of wasted affection,
affection never was wasted;
If it enrich not the heart
of another, its waters, returning
Back to their springs, like the rain,
shall fill them full of refreshment;
That which the fountain sends forth
returns again to the fountain."

—Henry Wadsworth Longfellow,
Evangeline (1847)

READING 2

your life can flow

There's something irresistible—almost magical—about fountains. Young and old alike can hardly pass by without dipping a finger into the shimmering wetness. Take a minute sometime and watch people as they pass by a fountain in a busy mall or park. What you see will probably make you smile.

It's as if there is an enormous magnet drawing fascinated children to come and splash. Stressed-out parents are pulled along behind them only to pause and peacefully watch their sons and daughters at play. From time to time they search their pockets for "wishing pennies" to give their kids, and when no one is looking, toss one in the water for themselves.

Irresistible.

There's a fountain in front of a church in the town where we live. This fountain was a joy to see and hear as its iridescent pillars of water constantly shot skyward—for the briefest of moments defying gravity—and then showered crystals down in a rainbow freefall. All year round, the steps surrounding it were not only a refuge for quiet prayers and silent meditation, but also a picturesque backdrop for generations of wedding photos, proud parents holding newly christened infants, and throngs of gap-toothed Sunday-schoolers receiving perfect attendance awards.

And at night, when no one else was about, probably more than a few couples held each other tight and whispered hushed words of love with that fountain's persistent song.

Poetic, huh?

It's really too bad that where it once stood so full of sparkling life, that wonderful fountain is now silent, dry, and empty except for a few seasons' worth of shaggy, dead vines coiling around the broken center column.

There's something profoundly unsettling about a dried-up fountain, isn't there? While flowing fountains speak of the richness of life, joy, and even romance; a dry fountain is a stark picture of death, sadness, and an emptiness you intuitively know does not belong there.

Fountains are *meant* to be full and constantly overflowing. It's what they're for. Anything else is just wrong!

Your Life as a Fountain

What if your life was like a fountain?

What if love, joy, hope, peace, grace—what if all of that flowed as freely in your life as sparkling water flows in a fountain? Overflowing. Abundant. Refreshing. Captivating.

It certainly sounds poetic, but could it possibly be true?

It is. It's a promise made to every person willing to accept it.

"I [Paul] ask him to strengthen you by his Spirit—not a brute strength but a glorious inner strength—that Christ will live in you as you open the door to invite him in. And I ask him that with both feet planted firmly on love, you'll be able to take in with all Christians the *extravagant dimensions* of Christ's love. *Reach out and experience the breadth! Test its length! Plumb the depths! Rise to the heights! Live full lives, full in the fullness of God.*

"God can do *anything*, you know—far more than you could ever imagine or guess or request *in your wildest dreams*! He does it not by pushing us around but by working within us, his Spirit deeply and gently within us" (EPHESIANS 3:16-20, *The Message*, emphasis added).

When you become a friend of Jesus—when you believe so fully in his love—you're able to experience life to the fullest. Life as it was meant to be: full of relationship, love, purpose, adventure, and fulfillment.

It's hard to imagine a world where all our needs for acceptance, friendship, achievement, and love aren't merely met, but continually overflowing...and, in turn, pouring into the lives of those around us. But this intriguing offer is repeated several times throughout the Bible—you'll recognize it here in this encounter between Jesus and a weary woman at the town well.

Put yourself in that poor woman's dusty sandals for a moment and try to consider what must have been going through her head as Jesus pointed down to the bottom of the deep well she was standing next to and said:

"Everyone who drinks this water will get thirsty again and again. Anyone who drinks the water I give will never thirst—not ever. The water I give will be an artesian spring within, gushing fountains of endless life" (JOHN 4:13-14, *The Message*).

Your first reaction probably goes something like this: "Uh oh! This guy must be nuts! I've seen lots of crazy people who talk to themselves and say outrageous things to passersby, and this is definitely more than a little weird."

And yet, there's something disturbingly sane about the look in this stranger's eyes and the earnestness in his voice. He doesn't look particularly scary; so you decide to play along. What have you got to lose anyway? After all, you're tired of the sweaty routine of lugging heavy water jars across town in the blistering, noonday heat, and the idea of his magical "living water" sounds pretty appealing right about now.

With just a tiny edge of sarcasm in your voice, you say, "Sir, give me this water so I won't ever get thirsty, won't ever have to come back to this well again!" (JOHN 4:15, *The Message*).

You're startled when, moments later, this man reveals prophetic talents, telling you things about yourself that he couldn't possibly know. For a moment you consider the possibility that he actually is a prophet...but only for a moment, because now he is telling you that he is the Messiah. *The Messiah!* The long-awaited person sent from God, the hero you've been told about since childhood. Could it be true? You drop your jar and run into the village to share this shocking news with anyone you can find...

Nearly 2,000 years have passed since this encounter at Sychar's village well, and people who say they believe in Jesus are nearly everywhere these days. Maybe you know some and maybe you are one, either way the question we have for you is the same: *Are you experiencing this endless life, this gushing fountain within you that Jesus promised?*

Is your life richly flowing with peace? power? passionate purpose? romance?

Or are you more like that dried-up fountain, living with a growing sense of inner dryness, apathy, and dissatisfaction?

Four Levels of Your Spiritual Fountain

So go ahead and imagine your life *is* a fountain. Specifically, the old-fashioned, four-tiered kind of fountain, with a tall column in the center carrying the water upward before it cascades down into four bowls below. These four bowls represent different types of relationships in your life—relationships implied in Christ's last words here on earth: "You will receive power when the Holy Spirit comes on you; and you will be my witnesses in *Jerusalem*, and in all *Judea* and *Samaria*, and to *the ends of the earth*" (ACTS 1:8, NIV, emphasis added).

So let's break it down. First things first: The disciples had to be filled with the Spirit of God. It's a mysterious thing, but we've been promised the same power: Everyone who has a relationship with Jesus is given power, wisdom, and insight when God sends his Spirit to them as a counselor and guide. The central column of the fountain is the Holy Spirit in *your* life. Just as the central column fills the fountain, so, too, the Holy Spirit wants to fill every one of your relationships with God's love, joy, and wonder.

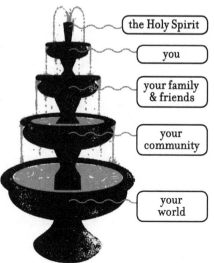

- the Holy Spirit
- you
- your family & friends
- your community
- your world

The first bowl that catches and distributes the power of the Spirit is **your relationship with God.** Following the pattern from Acts 1:8, it represents your personal "Jerusalem"—where you go to connect with God. Back when Jesus and the disciples were alive, Jerusalem was where Jews went to be close to God. From the time every Jew was knee-high to their local rabbi, they learned that if you wanted to hear the voice of God, worship him, talk to him, or serve him, you had to go to Jerusalem—to the temple. But Jesus changed all that. Now that Jesus has come, there's no longer any need to travel to a temple built with human hands. Because of his death, Jesus made it possible for every single person on earth to have a more direct, personal, and intimate relationship with God—no matter what city you're in (we'll dig into this more in Week 2). So that first bowl—your Jerusalem, your friendship with God—is the key bowl. It has to be filled up and overflowing first, *before* any of the other bowls can get any water.

Once you have a relationship with God, the first and most natural place his Spirit will overflow is going to be your home. So the second bowl of the fountain is **your relationship with family and friends.** For the disciples, *Judea* was home base. They knew it the way your great-grandparents knew their hometown. They understood the personalities and idiosyncrasies of the locals and knew all the inside jokes. Of course, on the flip side, the people of Judea knew the disciples just as well...and they were carefully (and even critically) watching the disciples to see if being with Jesus had really changed them. We'll explore this area in more detail during Week 3.

The third tier of the fountain represents how the Spirit flows into **your relationship with the community**—especially the people with whom you have little or no natural connection. For the disciples, *Samaria* was a nearby region they hated traveling through. They'd grown up thinking of folks who lived there as "not our kind of people." So they had generally ignored or shunned the Samaritans until Jesus taught them better (that woman at the well—she was a Samaritan). During Week 4, we'll zero in on how to love and connect with the people in your community (even those who aren't like you).

The last and largest bowl the Spirit wants to fill with love and life is **your relationship with the world.** When the disciples heard the words *"the ends of the earth,"* they were probably thinking of far away Roman provinces like Gaul or Britannia—places where rumors described savage barbarians wearing uncured animal skins and wielding fierce weapons, weapons they were more than willing to use at the slightest offense. So, in their minds, not exactly the most pleasant place to visit. The very idea of sharing God's love with such scary, non-Jewish people must have been more than a little upsetting. But God's love is meant for all people, and in Week 5 we'll help you identify and overcome any apprehensions you may have about bringing God's love to the ends of the earth.

Whoever You Are...

Maybe it's hard for you to imagine your life as a fountain in which each of these key areas is overflowing with richness. The truth is that it's hard for most people to believe that. The world around us—from magazines, to movies, to the Jones' next door—works hard to convince us that the true way to happiness is accumulating stuff, gaining advantages, and climbing ladders. The idea of being generous instead of stingy, of being outward-focused instead of self-focused, of trusting God instead of taking control...well, it seems counterintuitive. How can you be satisfied and fulfilled if you're constantly giving instead of taking?

But *that* water—the water of stuff, advantages, and ladders—never seems to satisfy for long. It's not long before we're thirsty again...before we want more stuff...before we need the next raise...before we're hunting for the next good deal. How different from the water that Jesus promises—water that when we drink of it, we'll never be thirsty again...we'll have more than we need...we'll overflow.

So whoever you are and whatever your struggles, whether you think of yourself as a friend of Christ or if—like the woman at the well—you're just hoping what he said might possibly be true, a most refreshing experience is right around the corner. Your life and the lives of those around you are about to change for the better. In the words of Saint Augustine, "God is more anxious to bestow his blessings on us than we are to receive them." God thirsts for *you* to experience your life as the overflowing fountain he created it to be. God longs to see the delight in your eyes as he gives you the desires of your heart (PSALM 37:4).

"If *anyone* is thirsty, let him come to me and drink. *Whoever* believes in me, as the Scripture has said, streams of living water will flow from within him" (JOHN 7:37-38, NIV, emphasis added).

getting your **feet wet**

Overflowing life as we've described it may sound nice, but what does it mean to you? Personalize it—make it more specific and concrete—by finishing the thoughts below. Let each of these openings spark your imagination and help you envision what abundant, overflowing life could look like in your relationships.

• I would know my relationship with God was overflowing with life if...

• I would know my relationships with family and friends were overflowing with life if...

• I would know my relationship with my community was overflowing with life if...

• I would know my relationship with the world was overflowing with life if...

the **reflection** *pool*

>> Are you an overflowing fountain? a clogged-up fountain? a barely-trickling fountain? a totally dried-up fountain? Describe your life in the context of fountain imagery.

>> What circumstances and emotions have led to the state of your fountain?

>> Do you believe that God can make your life and your relationships like an overflowing fountain? Why or why not? If not, what would make you believe?

"WHATEVER IS GOOD AND PERFECT COMES TO US FROM GOD OUR FATHER, WHO CREATED ALL THE LIGHTS IN THE HEAVENS. HE NEVER CHANGES OR CASTS A SHIFTING SHADOW."

—JAMES 1:17

"Praise God from whom all blessings flow; Praise him all creatures here below; Praise him above ye heavenly host; Praise Father, Son, and Holy Ghost. Amen."

—Thomas Ken,
Bishop of Bath and Wells

READING 3

blessings flow

If you look up the word *blessing* in the dictionary, you'll find out that it's *an indication of God's special favor or protection*. So when you say "God bless you" after someone sneezes, at least technically you're asking God to guard that person from harm and enrich the person's general well-being. Of course most of us don't really think through all of that after someone sneezes—the blessings we pronounce on others these days are primarily meaningless social conventions rather than heartfelt prayers.

God's blessings on you are another story altogether.

OK, let's get personal because God's blessings to you are just that— *personal*. In other words, they're created exactly for you—for your needs, your personality, and your desires. A blessing you've been craving all your life might mean nothing at all to someone else. And something that's "no big deal" to you might be the cherished treasure another has been longing for. It's like that perfect gift…there are some gifts that you open and then politely say, "That's nice." But there are other gifts that cause you to shout, "Yes! It's exactly what I've always wanted!" Those are the blessings God gives—the ones you've always wanted…whether you knew it or not.

Here's something Dave recently witnessed—a story that includes a tailor-made blessing straight from God:

> John is a pastor who'd been sent all the way from a remote part of Kenya to complete some of our training in Ohio. Soon after John arrived, he got a call from his brother back home in Kenya. From the look on John's face, it was clear he'd just received terrible news. Dave's wife, Pam, thought maybe someone close to him had died until Pastor John related this awful news: "Bandits have come in the night and taken my family's milk cow."
>
> It may not sound like a big deal to you. However, in the famine stricken area where John's from, that one cow was all that stood between John's family, the eleven orphans he had adopted, and almost certain starvation. By the time he finished talking, Pam knew she had to do something right away. Minutes later, normally frugal Pam was already in her car on the way to the Western Union office to wire John's family enough money (out of her own pocket) to buy a top-quality milk cow. Meanwhile, within 10 minutes of letting some of the other conference attendees know of his need, John had more than enough money to buy three cows!
>
> Though John felt certain God had wanted him to come to America, he'd been deeply concerned for his family and for his little village ever since he'd left. Overwhelmed by the immediate and generous response from people he'd never even met, John tearfully reflected, "If I had been home, I would have fought those bandits to try and stop them from stealing the cow…and I probably would have been killed. God is so good. I trusted him enough to come here…now he has saved both my family and me!"
>
> John didn't use the extra money God had provided to buy two more cows. No, he gave away all the rest to teachers in his village school—teachers who hadn't been paid in over a year! "God has blessed me," Pastor John explained, "How could I do any less for them?"

The blessings John received weren't just concerned words, they were also compassionate actions that flowed to him in his hour of need, and then overflowed from him to bless many others. Maybe that's what James was getting at when he wrote, "Whatever is good and perfect comes to us from God our Father, who created all the lights in the heavens" (JAMES 1:17).

Our heavenly Father delights in pouring down both "good gifts" and "perfect gifts" into our lives. Material things such as food, money, laptop computers, plasma screen TVs, and even *cows* are good gifts. While they last, these gifts provide for our temporary needs, but they're certainly not perfect—eventually they wear off, get lost, break, or even die. A perfect gift is one that can't be stolen, keeps on working no matter what, and never, ever fails. The only force in the universe that fits that bill is *God's perfect love for you.*

God Wants to Pour Out His Favor

Take a look at one of the Bible's most comprehensive lists of blessings in Deuteronomy 28:1-14.

According to this passage, God says he wants to pour out his *favor...*

≈ In your city
≈ In your country
≈ On your children
≈ On your crops
≈ On your land
≈ On the young of your livestock
≈ On the calves of your herds
≈ On the lambs of your flocks
≈ On your baskets
≈ On your bowls
≈ On your coming in
≈ On your going out
≈ In your battles

≈ In your barns
≈ In your workplaces
≈ In the respect you get from others
≈ In offspring from your animals
≈ In crops from your land
≈ In timely rain
≈ On your work
≈ On your finances
≈ On your leadership
≈ On your status
≈ In every good thing

Believe it or not, this is an abbreviated list! These are some seriously great blessings that cover the entire spectrum from urban to rural, family to farm animals, kitchen utensils to careers.

God wants to generously pour out his blessings on each of us who genuinely asks, seeks, and knocks on his door (MATTHEW 7:7; LUKE 11:9; JOHN 16:24; REVELATION 3:20). As Pastor John's experience illustrates, this doesn't mean that we'll be immune to famine, natural disasters, and other problems that affect those around us. No. It just means that God will never stop loving us or trying to pour rich blessings into our lives—even in the midst of hardship.

We don't want to be misinterpreted here. Perhaps you've heard preachers encouraging their followers to treat God like a kind of giant "vending machine in the sky," dispensing big bank accounts and BMWs. As some tell it, all you have to do in order to get something out of the vending machine is put money into the slot—by donating to *their* ministries. And guess what, *the more you give*, the *more you'll get*. If the diamond rings on some preachers' fingers—and the shiny rides in their garages—are any indication, too many people are buying this message.

Then there's the equally unbiblical (and all-American) idea that blessings are the natural result of hard work. In this view, the more diligently you apply yourself, and the better you do, the more favor you'll *earn* from God. This "gospel" of hard work naturally appeals to successful high achievers, but it's completely at odds with the picture God has given us. "To him who is thirsty," he proclaims, "I will give to drink *without* cost from the spring of the water of life" (REVELATION 21:6b, NIV, emphasis added). In other words, if you thirst for more of God's favor, you can have it for free—no donations or hard work required. All God is looking for is thirst!

Though many of the good things God wants to give us are material, that's certainly not all he has for us—not by a long shot. Stop and think for a minute about Jesus and his 12 closest followers as they walked the earth together. That's just it...*they walked*. It's pretty clear they weren't cruising along from town to town in stylish carriages or chariots. The only time Jesus is ever pictured riding during his ministry is on the back of a lowly baby donkey (MATTHEW 21:5). He and his entourage didn't stay in fine hotels or fancy villas. Matthew and Luke both record him saying, "Foxes have dens to live in, and birds have nests, but the Son of Man has no place even to lay his head" (MATTHEW 8:20; LUKE 9:58).

Franco Zeffirelli's famous 1977 movie, *Jesus of Nazareth*, captures this truth well in one scene when it pictures Jesus waking up one morning from a sound night's sleep...on a sidewalk in Jerusalem! One of the disciples wakes him up saying, "Master, someone is here who needs to see you!" Although thousands sat at his feet to listen to his teachings, and powerful leaders came to beg his advice, Jesus made his bed on the street like a homeless person. And according to his own words, that's what he was.

Yet none of us would say that Jesus wasn't blessed. Though he wasn't wealthy, Jesus had exactly what he needed...and all that he desired.

An Extreme Makeover

Whether you are rich or poor, God wants to bless you both spiritually and materially. Paul writes in Ephesians 3:20, "Now all glory to God, who is able, through his mighty power at work within us, to accomplish infinitely more than we might ask or think." Though you might be able to think up some pretty spectacular ways for God to bless you, our experience tells us that what God has in mind for you is even better than you could imagine! To use a pop-culture reference, God wants to bowl you over with the supernatural equivalent of *Extreme Makeover: Home Edition*. In case you've never seen or heard of it, this popular TV series showcases a team of professional designers, contractors, and hundreds of volunteers as they remodel the house of a deserving family. But they don't just simply lay new tile or knock down a few walls; they take enormous pains to build what's basically a completely new house—one in which every family member's wildest dreams can come true.

Every show begins the same way: The design team—in their gleaming, million-dollar tour bus—shows up at some tiny, dilapidated hovel. Tragic music plays as the host takes viewers on a tour of the terrible conditions the family has endured. Then they send the family away on a luxury cruise or extravagant Disneyland vacation while the designers go to work transforming the family's barely habitable house into a luxurious dream home—in just seven days. On the seventh day, the team parks the designers' tour bus in front of the now breathtaking house, and then all the family's neighbors and friends gather out in front of the bus and cheer as the family arrives. Now all that stands between the family and their incredible new dream home is a huge bus. And everyone begins to cry out together, "Move that bus!"

For us, the real fun of the show is watching the designers lovingly create rooms and experiences, each one premeditated to blow the minds of the family members. We think it's a cool picture of what God does for each one of us. God is anxiously and eagerly waiting to reveal a life different and *far better* than anything you've been hoping for—a life he has tailor-made just for you, a life he knows is exactly what you've always wanted, a life that will blow your mind. All you have to do is honestly believe in God's love for you…and then shout, "Move that bus!"

Doug's Extreme Makeover

We have a friend named Doug who leads a growing church in Dayton, Ohio. When he first started, some might have said that Doug's speaking style wasn't quite ready for prime time. But the great thing about Doug is that he has allowed God to do the kind of "extreme makeover" we've been talking about in his life. You can tell what's happened to him just by listening to his answering machine. It says something like: "I'm not here right now because I'm out doing all kinds of good things for all kinds of people and having more fun than a human being should have. Go ahead and leave a message and I'll call you back." Doug's extremely generous attitude has helped his little church grow into one of the largest, most powerful, and most enjoyable places in town.

In fact, his church likes to throw big parties they call "Fun Fests." These Fun Fests often draw as many as 4,500 neighbors from the community for a time of hanging out, eating, playing games, and, in general, having a wonderful time with family and friends. The best thing about Doug's church is that it's not about Doug. It's not about his speaking ability or his personality or even the cool things Doug does. Instead, Doug's church is about receiving so much from God that Doug and his whole congregation can't—and don't want to—contain it. So God's love and blessings constantly flow out of the church—touching and enriching more lives every day.

Doesn't that sound great?

We know that for many reading this book it's hard to imagine going to a church, or for that matter, living a life like Doug's. As far as you may be concerned, if there is a blessing-bus waiting out there for you, it has yet to pull up at your life's front door. Perhaps you're worn out from struggling to keep your head above water at work. Maybe you're so lonely and depressed you can't imagine that God, or anyone else, cares what happens to you. Or perhaps you've stood helpless as the wonderful life you thought you had disintegrated before your eyes. To use an image from the last chapter, if your life is meant to flow like a fountain, right now there's something seriously wrong with the pump. If this describes your situation even a little bit, the next chapter is all about things that can clog the inflow and outflow of blessings in your life.

getting your feet wet

Sometimes we forget or take the good things that have happened in our lives for granted. Here's an idea that will help you remember. Find a pickle jar or similar transparent container, a permanent fine-point marker, and some small, smooth stones you can write on (or you can just use scraps of paper). Take a minute and ask God to remind you of some of the blessings you've experienced in your life during the last year. As you think of each one, thank God for it. Then write a brief description of the blessing on one of the rocks and put it in the jar.

Leave the jar in your kitchen or somewhere you pass by every day. As blessings flow into your life, give thanks, write what happened on one of these "stones of remembrance," and toss it into the jar. If you keep it up, you'll be amazed at how quickly your jar fills up and overflows.

the reflection pool

>> What do you immediately consider "blessings" in your life? Why?

>> Describe a time you were given a "blessing in disguise." How did that blessing impact your life? How does that blessing reveal God's intimate love for you?

>> Consider Matthew 7:7-8. What are the implications of these verses for your life?

"THE THIEF DOES NOT COME
EXCEPT TO STEAL, AND TO
KILL, AND TO DESTROY.
I HAVE COME THAT THEY
MAY HAVE LIFE, AND
THAT THEY MAY HAVE IT
MORE ABUNDANTLY."

—JOHN 10:10 (NKJV)

"But enough about me.
Let's talk about you.
What do you think of me?"

—former New York Mayor, Ed Koch

READING 4

the water thief

The Bible quote above is part of a conversation Jesus had with some rather uptight religious people called Pharisees. These Pharisees stood in outspoken opposition to Jesus' ministry. To give you a little background, the Pharisees taught that only those who meticulously followed the narrowest interpretations of all the Old Testament laws and Jewish traditions could earn God's blessings. Depending on how short you fell of total perfection, God might not only withhold his favor, he would punish you—causing your crops to fail or visiting disaster, disease, and ill fortune on you, your children, and even your children's children. It was a pretty simple idea: If you were rich, healthy, and prosperous, God was blessing you for your good deeds; if you were poor, sick, or struggling, it was because you or some ancestor ticked off God.

An amazing number of people who are sincerely trying to follow Christ's teachings are unconsciously operating from ideas that have more in common with the Pharisees' teachings (and the Hindu philosophy of good and bad *karma*) than anything Jesus taught. When you assume everything that's wrong with your life is your own fault—or society's, your parents', or even an ex-spouse's fault—or when you assume that to get God's blessings, you have to be perfect—then you're missing the point of what Jesus is saying in John 10:10. Jesus is very clear that there's more to it than that. For one thing, there's a *supernatural thief* doing everything he can think of to steal, kill, and utterly destroy the flow of blessings God intends for your life.

You know this thief. He's been with you since the earliest days of your childhood, stealing words of encouragement from your heart and leaving blame, condemnation, and suspicion in their place. His snaky voice has always been there in the background, whispering. See if you recognize it:

You don't belong...

If you were more like your brother, you'd be successful...

That co-worker is out to get you...

Nobody appreciates you...

This thief is subtle, devious, and brutal in his never-ending quest to rob you of every drop of whatever is true, whatever is honorable, whatever is right, whatever is pure, whatever is lovely, whatever is admirable, excellent, or praiseworthy in your life (PHILIPPIANS 4:8). The Bible compares him to a roaring lion prowling around looking for someone to devour (1 PETER 5:8). And unfortunately, *that someone is you.*

But there's good news—you can fight this thief by desperately clinging to Jesus' promises. Read the second part of John 10:10: Jesus says he came so you can have life—and *not* the life of "quiet desperation" that Henry David Thoreau declared as the lot of man—Jesus came to give you *abundant* life.

Look up the word *abundant* in your trusty thesaurus and you'll find words like *copious, ample, rich, lavish, generous, plentiful, bounteous, overflowing,* and *large*. Those are some good words. We like to think Jesus came down to earth because he wanted you to be "livin' large" in every way that really matters. You may have a hard time imagining it, but financial prosperity is only a minor element of the riches Jesus came to give you. By the time you're done reading this book, we hope you'll discover deeper elements of abundance that can overflow into your life in a way that wealth never could.

How Do Blessings Flow?

One of Steve's favorite words in any language comes from the Norwegian translation of "abundant life" from John 10:10. The Norwegian word is *over-flod* (pronounced oover-floood). Don't you just love the sound of it? If your kids have ever left the water running in the bathtub or your toilet has ever overflowed, you know something of what it's like to have *copious, ample, rich, lavish, abounding* amounts of water all over the floor. But what does overflowing *life* look like?

Try to imagine being filled with *all the fullness of God!* We're talking about so much love, so much joy, and so much power that you could never, ever contain it. And guess what? You aren't meant to contain it; you are designed to be *constantly* filled up with, and *constantly* pouring out God's love and blessing. Just as a tree is intricately designed down to the last tiny leaf to grow upward toward the sun, you are created to be a channel through which God's blessings can flow. You were meant to pass on the healing and refreshing water he gives to you, and pour it into other lives.

Wait one blessed minute here! Are you saying God is only filling me up so I can turn around and give it all away? That doesn't make sense! And, if you listen to the Thief, it doesn't. But if you listen to God, you'll find out why it's the best way. Here's what the Bible says:

"All praise to God, the Father of our Lord Jesus Christ. God is our merciful Father and the source of all comfort. He comforts us in all our troubles so that we can comfort others. When they are troubled, we will be able to give them the same comfort God has given us. For the more we suffer for Christ, the more God will shower us with his comfort through Christ" (2 CORINTHIANS 1:3-5).

It's that oover-floood thing again! First, whatever troubles we may have, God gives us comfort from his unlimited supply. So when we encounter others with troubles, we can pass on the comfort we received from God. And, yeah, this would be a bad deal for us if God's comfort supply could ever run short, which is why it's one of the Thief's key strategies to undermine our trust in God's ability to meet our needs. When we don't believe that God is willing or able to give us what we need, we start putting our own interests ahead of others' and stockpiling things for ourselves. Although God created us to *love God and people and to use things,* the Thief convinces us to reverse that order. We start *loving things* and *using God or people* as a means to get what we want. In doing this, we not only destroy the flow of good things God intends for us, we open the door to all sorts of evil.

Here's the story of Dr. Bob—a very smart and successful man who fell victim to the lies of the Thief.

Bob was born to Jewish parents during the Nazi occupation of Poland. When Bob was an infant, his family fled Poland for the United States, but when they arrived, their immigration visas were denied and they were forced to travel south to Cuba, the closest country that would take them in. So they settled in Cuba during the turbulent years preceding Castro's revolution. By the time he was a teenager, Bob and his family were war refugees again, only this time they *were* able to immigrate to the U.S.

During all these tribulations, the Thief was working overtime in Bob's heart—convincing Bob that he didn't fit in anywhere. He was that "foreign boy" in Cuba, and an "outsider" in an American society dominated by white, Anglo-Saxon Protestants. For Bob, the result of these lies was a nearly insatiable drive to prove himself and teach every snob who looked down on him a lesson. Hiding his Cuban accent as best he could, Bob earned a coveted spot at Johns Hopkins Medical School, and then completed his residency as Chief of Pediatrics at Yale. Though his academic and professional success surpassed most of his classmates, Bob still wasn't satisfied. His thriving practice, fine reputation, beautiful family, and large home were not enough. He was obsessed with proving himself through wealth, expensive things, high-powered friends, and beautiful women. When his first marriage eventually crumbled, he threw himself into the singles scene with a vengeance, appropriately christening his new party boat "The Hedonist."

The more it looked like Dr. Bob had it all, the emptier he was inside. You see, the Thief had fostered his insatiable hunger for success *specifically to steal away every good relationship Bob had ever had.*

But the story doesn't end there.

Recently a man said this about Bob: "He's so different from the man I remember from 25 years ago. *I don't think I've ever seen anyone so completely transformed!* He was so driven back then; all he ever talked about was money. I think he spent more time talking with his stockbroker than he did with his wife and children."

You see, as Bob's second marriage was heading for the rocks, he and his new wife, Janis, decided to try something neither had done since childhood—they went to church. While they were there, they signed up for a class called *Renewing the Mind*. This course showed Bob and Janis how to expose and overcome the lies of the Thief. As Dr. Bob related memories from his childhood he wept—not just in grief, but because for the first time he had begun to understand the true abundance God had in mind for him.

Bob and Janis recently celebrated 17 years of a marriage that literally overflows with love and joy. It spills over into the lives of the struggling couples with whom they volunteer, to the needy children whom they provide free medical supplies and treatment, and, for the last 10 years, to the people in the struggling churches of Cuba!

You may be wondering why Bob or anyone else would believe the Thief in the first place. And nobody would if he wasn't such a good liar. The Thief is incredibly adept at taking your life circumstances and twisting them to reflect a negative reality. Just as the Thief convinced Bob that he was an outsider and needed to constantly prove himself in order to be worthy, the Thief lies to us all. Maybe you're not exactly like Bob—you don't feel the need to prove yourself—but maybe instead the Thief has convinced you that your spouse isn't meeting your needs and you're a victim of a bad marriage. Or maybe the Thief has twisted your perception of life so that you're depressed and hopeless. Or perhaps the Thief has used one of his favorite tricks and trapped you in a pattern of apathy and indifference—a pattern that has led you to settle for a life you never wanted. The Thief has an arsenal of weapons, each one meant to block the flow of blessings in your life and eventually turn you into a dried-up fountain.

A Life That Sucks

Does a working fountain dry up when it continually yields its water to flow out from one tier to another? Of course not! But try to imagine what might take place if somehow one of the tiers became convinced it had to stop its outward flow and keep all of "its water" to itself. Whether that tier acted from fear, ignorance, or selfishness, the harmony of its design is disrupted when the flow to any part of a fountain is blocked. Eventually water will stop flowing into that tier—because if a tier is full of water and it's not going to let any flow out, then there's no reason for that tier to have any more water. Even with an inexhaustible source of living water, this is the kind of thing that leads to the tragedy of dried-up fountains. And the Thief rejoices.

The result of the Thief's deception is very plain to see: When you dance to the Thief's tune, your life begins to suck in instead of flow out.

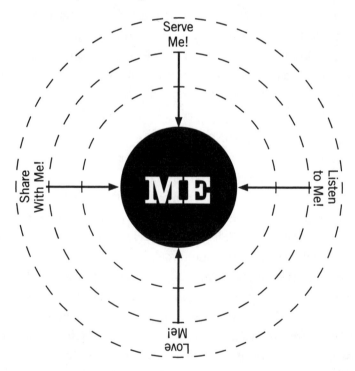

From God's perspective, a life that is beginning to "suck" looks something like the diagram shown here. Instead of the flow of God's Spirit pouring out and lavishly overflowing into the lives of others, Self is in the center attempting to inhale or vacuum what it needs from everyone around it. Having forsaken God's spring of living water, the Self attempts to beg, borrow, or steal what it needs from other humans. The result is an increasingly empty, increasingly dried-up, increasingly self-focused life. And if you pay attention to many of the people around you, you'll hear them subtly (or not so subtly) crying out, *"Listen to me! Love me! Share with me! Serve me!"* If you listen honestly, one of the voices you may hear is your own.

If your soul has ever been duped by the water Thief—and since the Garden of Eden we have all experienced this at one time or another—you'll appreciate seeing some of his most sinister and effective strategies exposed in the next reading.

getting your **feet wet**

What comes to mind when you think about what the Thief has stolen, killed, or destroyed in your life?

Take a minute to go into your kitchen or bathroom and look at the drain in the bottom of your sink. Think of all the good things that slipped through your fingers as a result of the Thief's lies in your life. Now turn the water on and think about the abundant life Jesus has for you. If you want to, tell God the deepest desire of your heart by saying something like, "God, I'm really thirsty for more. Here is my heart's desire." Then take a big drink.

"Delight yourself in the Lord and he will give you the desires of your heart"
(PSALM 37:4, NIV).

the **reflection** *pool*

>> Be honest: What are the desires of your heart? How do you think those desires compare to the desires God has for your life?

>> Describe a time you really felt like the Thief was attacking you and lying to you. Were you successful in fighting off the Thief? Why or why not?

>> After reading this chapter, how do you think you can fight the Thief in the future?

READING 5

the judas factor

How do you figure the value of anything? As every salesperson, entrepreneur, or stockbroker will tell you, *value is determined by what a buyer is willing to pay.* The people who run eBay and similar Internet auction sites have made tremendous fortunes because they know this truth—they realize that one person's trash is literally another's treasure. Perhaps you've seen some of the improbable "bargains" that sellers are offering online.

One of our all-time favorite eBay auctions was for a UFO detector...with AA batteries included. Its Brazilian manufacturer advertised that the UFO detector could detect minute fluctuations in the earth's magnetic field caused by visitations from alien spacecraft. Unfortunately, accuracy was not 100 percent guaranteed due to the fact that the propulsion systems of UFOs are not all the same. The UFO detector went for the final sale price of $135.03. Then there was the grilled cheese sandwich said to bear the image of the Virgin Mary that sold for $28,000 and a "haunted" walking cane that went for $65,000.

One eBay seller even offered to reveal "the meaning of life" online. We're not talking about the Monty Python movie here, but the ultimate secret of existence—the secret that philosophers and theologians have been seeking since the dawn of civilization. The seller said he'd finally figured it out, and now he was auctioning it off to the highest bidder. Even with eight bids, the answer to life's greatest question didn't fetch much. But who knows? It may have been the best $3.26 the winning bidder ever spent.

The thing is, every single buyer—even the one who bought Britney Spears' chewing gum for $263 and the potato chip shaped like a cowboy boot for over $1,000—thought he or she was getting value for the money. It may not make sense to you, but from the buyers' perspective, when they hit that ENTER key they believed what they were getting was worth every penny.

If it sounds a little crazy to you—that people would pay good money for such ridiculous stuff—then imagine what God must think when he surveys the choices we make every day. The Bible tells us that at the end of the day, "...the wages of sin is death, but the free gift of God is eternal life through Christ Jesus our Lord" (Romans 6:23). It sounds like a no-brainer. Of course we'd rather be given eternal life, right? Apparently not considering that, for weird reasons of our own, we often choose the Thief's idea of a "bargain" over God's free gift. In the moment, it feels pretty darn good to indulge in actions we know are wrong—even if we know they're guaranteed to produce terrible consequences in the end. The truth is, every act of lying, stealing, cheating, or selfishness ever committed almost certainly seemed "worth it" at the time the person did it. And that's how the Thief tricks us.

Though we might not like to admit it, all of us have—at one time or another—freely chosen to go against what God says (and what we know in our hearts) is right. Like Adam and Eve (and every single person since—except Jesus), you've done things God has forbidden or you've chosen not to do things you knew were right. The Apostle Paul underlines this 100 percent failure rate by saying, "For *everyone* has sinned; we *all* fall short of God's glorious standard"(Romans 3:23, emphasis added). And "No one does good, not a single one" (Romans 3:12b).

We've blown it and continue to blow it for one big reason: *We're easy to deceive*. The chief tool of the Thief is *deception*. In John 8:44b, Jesus describes his tactics saying, "He was a murderer from the beginning, not holding to the truth, for there is no truth in him. When he lies, he speaks his native language, for he is a liar and the father of lies" (NIV). For the world's oldest and slimiest deceiver, it's practically child's play to mess with our values...to get us thinking down is up, good is bad, richness is poverty...that trash is worth millions and that the true treasure is trash.

If you need an example, read the first few chapters of the Bible. God gave Adam and Eve all of paradise for their personal playground. God gave them all the fish of the sea, all the birds of the air, and every living creature and all of the plants that bear fruit except for one. In Genesis 1:31, God looked over the whole earth that he'd just given to one man and one woman and pronounced the whole thing "very good." Sounds *very* good to us! We're not talking about a few hundred measly mansions on a few thousand meager acres. Adam and Eve literally had *everything*—including what every soul hungers for: a perfect relationship with God!

But there sat the Thief dressed up as a serpent. He had a big challenge before him: He had to convince the jackpot winners of the universe's richest lotto that God was being stingy toward them. Unfortunately, the Thief is really good at being bad!

You know how that story ends. Adam and Eve were deceived into valuing the one thing they weren't supposed to have over all the billions of good things God had already given them. It's hard to figure out how anyone could be so badly bamboozled...*unless it has happened to you.*

Case in point: One Judas, called Iscariot, was an incredibly fortunate man. Judas was one of just 12 men in recorded history to spend nearly every waking hour of his life for three years with the living, breathing Son of God. Judas was probably as familiar with Jesus—his teachings, his moods, his every tone and inflection, even the funny sounds he made when he laughed— as you are with the idiosyncrasies of your best friend or spouse.

Imagine all the healings and miracles Judas witnessed. Judas must have tasted the water that had been turned to wine. He must have spoken with Lazarus after he returned from death and with the woman at the well when she took her entire village to hear Jesus. Judas was just feet away from Peter as he jumped out of the boat and walked on water with the Lord. Judas even let Jesus serve him by washing his feet. Even after being present for the greatest miracles of all time, even after hearing Jesus' life-changing words, even after seeing lives changed and perspectives shifted, even after all of that—Judas *still* didn't think he had enough. *The only person Judas could think of serving was Judas.*

At some point along the way, Judas had let the Thief cloud his mind and darken his understanding. Matthew tells the story as follows:

> Meanwhile, Jesus was in Bethany at the home of Simon, a man who had previously had leprosy. While he was eating, a woman came in with a beautiful alabaster jar of expensive perfume and poured it over his head.

> The disciples were indignant when they saw this. "What a waste of money," they said. "It could have been sold for a high price and the money given to the poor."

> But Jesus, aware of this, replied, "Why criticize this woman for doing such a good thing to me? You will always have the poor among you, but you will not always have me. She has poured this perfume on me to prepare my body for burial. I tell you the truth, wherever the Good News is preached throughout the world, this woman's deed will be remembered and discussed."

> Then Judas Iscariot, one of the twelve disciples, went to the leading priests and asked, "How much will you pay me to betray Jesus to you?" And they gave him thirty pieces of silver. From that time on, Judas began looking for an opportunity to betray Jesus.

(MATTHEW 26:6-16)

In John's account of Jesus being anointed with perfume, he identifies the woman pouring out the oil as Mary, the sister of Martha and Lazarus. He also specifically identifies Judas Iscariot as the disciple complaining, "That perfume was worth a year's wages. It should have been sold and the money given to the poor" (JOHN 12:4-5). John also adds a chilling bit of commentary about Judas saying, "[Judas] did not say this because he cared about the poor but because he was a thief; as keeper of the money bag, he used to help himself to what was put into it" (JOHN 12:6, NIV).

So what does this have to do with experiencing overflowing life? Well, here it is: Instead of listening to understand *why* Jesus was praising the woman, Judas focused inward. You could say his inner fountain was set on "suck" instead of "flow." Though on the surface Judas piously complained of waste and sanctimoniously spoke of giving to the poor, underneath he was chanting the inward-focused mantra he'd learned from the master Thief: *"What's in it for me?"*

Tragically, Judas didn't seem to grasp the completely unselfish act of love Mary had literally poured out on Jesus. What Judas' self-clouded, Thief-deceived mind did see was an embarrassing, inappropriate emotional display and a terrible waste of money (that he could put to "better" use).

The fragrant oil of nard Mary spilled was indeed very expensive. Imagine a year's wages, or the cost of a new Mercedes. Imagine cashing in your retirement plan and spending all of it on one single bottle of perfume. Honestly, if you did this, wouldn't some of your family members think seriously about calling the nice men in white coats to come and haul you away to a padded room? What if those same relatives saw you getting ready to pour out that $50,000 bottle of Chanel No. 5 on the head of your rabbi or pastor? Can't you just picture your sister Martha or uncle Ned diving through the air in slow motion to try to stop you—screaming *"Noooooooo!"*

If you're honest, you'll probably admit the whole scene sounds about as crazy to you as it did to Judas. Perhaps if your pastor had brought your brother back to life after four days of rotting in the grave—as Jesus had done for Mary's brother, Lazarus—then maybe this kind of extreme gesture would make a little more sense.

The thing is, Jesus not only praised Mary's gift he also accorded her one of the highest honors any person in Christian history has ever received. Jesus said that wherever his gospel was preached throughout the world, he wanted everyone to hear her story (MATTHEW 26:13). But why would Jesus say this?

It wasn't the money, or that Jesus was "really into" perfume. It was the utterly outward-focused love of her giving. There was nothing in it for Mary but the pure joy of showing her Lord what he meant to her. In an awful lot of human societies, talk is cheap and the people who praise you to your face will sometimes betray you in private. So there is something downright wonderful about demonstrating love in ways words could never communicate.

Mary's gift is even greater than most of us understand today. As the other Gospels tell the story, Mary didn't just anoint Christ's head with oil like an

Old Testament king or prophet. She stooped down to do what only the lowliest servants of her day were ever required to do. She washed his feet, and not just with soap and water, but with her own grateful tears. Then, scandalously to all but Jesus, she unbound her hair and dried his feet with it. If you grasp her utter abandonment, you may begin to understand why Jesus wanted Mary's story told over and over wherever his gospel went.

If this display of emotional and spiritual abandon makes you uncomfortable, you're certainly not alone. It's terribly shocking, ridiculously extravagant, and completely out of the ordinary. This is not the safe, homogenized religion many of us have come to expect—not by a long shot. Mary's is not the kind of story you tell if you like your religion cerebral, tame, or reasonable. She let go of the "What's in it for me?" attitude that ultimately drove Judas to betray Jesus. She not only understood the deep joy of receiving the overflowing love of Jesus, but also the fierce thrill of loving him back in the ways he cares about most.

Remember that verse about how we all fall short of God's glory? How about that one saying the wages of sin is death? Well, they're both true. And they both apply to every one of us; we've all fallen short of God's perfect standard, and we're all condemned to death. But, what Mary experienced—and what's true for all of us—is that Jesus came to change all that.

Jesus died the death we were condemned to die. He was completely innocent—having never sinned even once—and yet he paid the wages of our sins. And because of his love and his sacrifice, we can receive the gift of eternal life.

That's why Mary fell at Jesus' feet and poured an incredibly expensive bottle of perfume on his head. That's why people for centuries have given their lives to worship Jesus.

There is no value you can place on Jesus' sacrifice. It's priceless.

But, like Mary, you can show your love and gratitude.

If you're thirsty for a life less ordinary, more passionate, and unpredictably powerful, the next section will point you toward the biblical antidote to the disease of self-centeredness. If you place a high value on knowing God more deeply, then you'll like what's coming.

getting your **feet wet**

God places a high value on you. So much so that God sent his only Son to die so that God could have a personal relationship with you. That's the price God paid for your friendship—and God felt that price was "worth it."

What is your relationship with God worth to you?

Jesus said, "Where your treasure is, there your heart will be also" (LUKE 12:34, NIV). Mary's unselfish anointing of Jesus with her treasured perfume spoke volumes about how much her relationship with Jesus meant to her.

What do you treasure most in your life? Time? Money? Family? Friends?

How can you offer that treasure to God? Write some ideas in the space below:

....

....

....

....

....

....

....

....

....

If you can, visualize your treasure sitting in your cupped hands. Lift it up to God and ask, "If it's true you treasure me even more than I love what's here in my hands, let me experience and share that love."

the **reflection** *pool*

>> God believed a personal relationship with you was worth the cost of his Son's life. What kind of an emotional response does that trigger in you?

>> How can you use your treasures to worship God?

>> How might your life change if you experienced the powerful emotions of gratitude and love toward God that Mary must have been feeling?

Take *the plunge…dive into the deep end…swim down until your ears start to hurt—metaphorically speaking, of course.*

The truth is The Deep End experiences *are* meant to make you a little uncomfortable. They're meant to take you beyond where you've been, to help you see from a perspective you've never before experienced.

Each week, The Deep End experiences will challenge you to live what you've learned—to take what you've read this week from the safe confines of theory and into the uncertain realm of real life.

If your faith were a pool, these experiences would be the equivalent of slipping under that dividing rope, creeping forward until even your tiptoes no longer touch the bottom, and then swimming out toward deeper waters…

So go on and do it…dive into the deep end—by yourself, with your family, your group of friends, or even your whole church! You'll get wet, that's for sure, but your faith will never be the same!

the deep end

TAKE A WALK

It's your first week of *Outflow* and there's a lot to think about and to hope for. The next four weeks—your *Outflow* experience—is still a blank slate. God has great plans for you: to fill you up and to help you overflow into your friends, your family, your community, and your world. Use this Deep End experience to connect with God and to reflect on those plans.

By yourself or with your small group, determine four spots in your area that represent each tier of the fountain. For example, you might choose a quiet garden or walking trail to represent your relationship with God, a favorite hangout or restaurant to represent your friends and family, a busy spot such as a mall or park to represent your community, and a spot just outside of town to represent the world.

By yourself or with your group, make a journey to all four of these spots, stopping at each one to pray. While you're there, walk around the spot and ask God to fill you to overflowing with his love for the people represented there. Pray that God would move you and change your perspective for serving and loving these people in the next four weeks…and beyond. Seek God's desires for your life and the ways he can use you to reach his beloved people. Finally, stop and listen to the sounds of the people around you…and to the ways God is

group
discussion questions

Use these questions during your small-group time and dialogue together about the first week of Outflow *readings.*

>> How do you hope *Outflow* will affect your life personally? How about your hopes for how *Outflow* might change our group?

>> Reading 2 compares your life to a fountain. Would you say you are an overflowing fountain? a clogged-up fountain? a barely-trickling fountain? a totally dried-up fountain? Why? Describe your life as a fountain.

>> Describe a blessing God has given you. How did that blessing impact your life? How does that blessing reveal God's intimate love for you?

>> When have you felt most attacked by the Thief? How did God help you through that attack?

>> God believed a personal relationship with you was worth the cost of his Son's life. What kind of an emotional response does that trigger in you?

you

outward toward God

"No one has ever seen God.
But if we love each other,
God lives in us, and his love is
brought to full expression in us."

—1 JOHN 4:12

"Years ago my mother used to
say to me, she'd say, 'In this world, Elwood...
you must be oh so smart or oh so pleasant.'
Well, for years I was smart.
I recommend pleasant. And you may quote me."

—Elwood P. Dowd, from the movie *Harvey*

READING 6

jerusalem

Have you ever met someone who has an invisible friend? You know, *weird* people who spend lots of time having conversations with someone nobody else can see. You may think they're nutty, but where we come from, they're called Christians. If you are one, your invisible friend has a name—no, it's not Harvey—it's God and he is *very* real.

In case you don't get the reference, we're talking about the 1950 classic movie *Harvey* starring Jimmy Stewart as Elwood P. Dowd—a mild-mannered, pleasantly eccentric man whose best friend is named Harvey. The twist is that Harvey just happens to be an invisible, 6-foot-3½-inch tall, white rabbit. *Harvey* is one of our favorite movies precisely because it forces the audience to ask, "Who's crazy here? Is it the friendly, easy-going, and very generous Elwood? Or all the frustrated, unhappy people trying to force him into treatment?"

During the movie Elwood is taken to receive a treatment that's guaranteed to get him back in touch with "reality." The taxi driver who takes Elwood for this treatment stops to ponder the whole thing, saying, "I've brought them out here to get that stuff, and I've drove them home after they had it... On the way out here, they sit back and enjoy the ride. They talk to me; sometimes we stop and watch the sunset, and look at the birds fly. And sometimes we stop and watch the birds when there ain't no birds and look at the sunset when its raining. We have a swell time. And I always get a big tip."

In other words, a "crazy" person with an invisible friend, an open heart, and a generous attitude is still a wonderful companion to share a cab with. Those kinds of people see things others don't see, and dream dreams others dismiss as wishful thinking. In many ways they're a breath of fresh air in a stale and stuffy world.

In fact, we'd like to think of Christ's followers as cab passengers who have a relationship with a *real* invisible friend—a friend who allows them to transcend a lot of the ugly pettiness of the world, a friend who allows them to look beyond the "What's in it for me?" attitude. Call it "divine madness" or perhaps "divine sanity." Either way, life is much richer, more real, and less sinister with this invisible friend at our sides.

Take a look at history and you'll encounter lots of people over the centuries who've experienced the intimate, moment-by-moment relationship with God the Bible talks about. Once these folks encountered God, their lives were never "conventional" again. They weren't average or even slightly above average—their relationship with God made them extraordinary! George is a good example. He was born into slavery near the end of the American Civil War and began talking with the "invisible" God when he was just 10 years old.

"God just came into my heart one afternoon while I was alone in the loft of our big barn...that was my simple conversion, and I have tried to keep the faith," George wrote many years later.

As he grew to be a young man, George's passion to understand everything he could about God and his creation burned within him. He took long walks in the woods collecting and studying all sorts of plants and insects. Overcoming huge social obstacles, George pursued a level of education generally denied to ex-slaves. Eventually he even earned a Master's degree from Iowa State Agricultural College and spent 47 years on the faculty of the Tuskegee Institute in Tuskegee, Alabama.

If you've studied American history, perhaps you've already guessed we're talking about the great agriculturist and inventor George Washington Carver—the man who invented over 300 marketable products derived from peanuts. You may be able to name several of his peanut products, but what you may not know is that George Washington Carver was a man who loved God deeply and talked to God daily. And some of his greatest inventions were direct answers to a simple prayer that went like this: "Mr. Creator, why did you make the peanut?"

In addition to creating flour, instant coffee, shampoo, rubber, cosmetics, axle grease, mayonnaise, and hundreds of other products from peanuts, George's greatest joy was shaping the lives of innumerable students and introducing them to his unseen friend. He once wrote: "I want [my students] to find Jesus...How I long for each one to walk and talk with the Great Creator through the things He has created."

George's love and trust of the invisible God not only allowed him to conquer terrible poverty and racial prejudice in his own life but it helped him empower millions of other people to do the same. He lived the overflowing life that this book is all about!

George Washington Carver is just one of countless people who've lived uncommonly powerful lives with the help of this invisible friend. The book of Hebrews lists several of them and tells of how one of them, Moses, overcame his fear of the Pharaoh and saved his people from slavery "because he kept his eyes on *the one who is invisible*" (HEBREWS 11:27, emphasis added). Moses, George, and many others have come to know the invisible God as a protector, provider, and powerful friend—and have led great lives because of it.

Unfortunately, we've met plenty of other people who've lost or never had a vital connection with the invisible friend we're talking about. There is a parallel between their experiences and what Elwood's cab driver predicted would happen to Elwood once the treatment caused him to lose touch with *his* invisible friend. Here's what the cab driver said,

"Afterwards, uh oh, they crab, crab, crab. They yell at me. Watch the lights. Watch the brakes. Watch the intersection. They scream at me to hurry. They got no faith in me, or my buggy. Yet, it's the same cab, the same driver. And we're going back over the very same road. It's no fun. And no tips...After this he'll be a perfectly normal human being. And you know what stinkers they are!"

If you are tired of being a perfectly normal, self-focused "stinker," it's high time you were introduced to—or reacquainted with, or just reminded to pay more attention to—the invisible God who not only promises to "guide you into all truth" (JOHN 16:13a, NLT) but also to "never leave you nor forsake you" (DEUTERONOMY 31:8b, NIV).

Maybe you're still not sure whether or not God is real. Or maybe you're still questioning whether or not God is all the incredible things we've described. Or maybe the big question for you is how in the world to start this wonderful friendship with God. No matter what questions you're asking right now, the best way forward is to check God out for yourself. Go ahead and take him up on his invitation to come drinking. We're serious—it's the same offer we mentioned earlier:

"If anyone is thirsty, let him come to me and drink. Whoever believes in me, as the Scripture has said, streams of living water will flow from within him" (JOHN 7:37b-38, NIV).

What Does It Mean to Have a "Relationship"?

Maybe you've heard someone talking about "getting to know God in a personal way." Of course, most of these people will freely admit they've never seen God with their eyes, heard God with their ears, smelled God with their noses, or touched God with their fingers. And yet they speak as if relating directly with the all-powerful, all-knowing Creator is the most natural thing in the world. It's a truly audacious claim if we've ever heard one! And it's no less audacious for being 100 percent true.

It may sound odd to those who haven't experienced it, but you can actually get to know God in some of the same ways you get to know human friends. Of course, instead of using only your five senses to interact with God, you have to learn to *see and hear with your spirit*. When Jesus asked some of the people who followed him, "Do you have eyes but fail to see, and ears but fail to hear?" (MARK 8:18a, NIV), Jesus was talking about spiritual blindness and deafness. In another passage he spoke to people whose spiritual eyes and ears were wide open, saying to them, "Blessed are your eyes because they see, and your ears because they hear" (MATTHEW 13:16, NIV). It's why the Apostle Paul prays "that the *eyes of your heart* may be enlightened in order that you may know the hope to which he has called you, the riches of his glorious inheritance in the saints, and his incomparably great power for us who believe" (EPHESIANS 1:18-19, NIV, emphasis added).

The good news is that God is ready to awaken and increase your spiritual senses if you ask him to. As Jesus said in Matthew 7:8, "Everyone who asks, receives. Everyone who seeks, finds. And to everyone who knocks, the door will be opened" (NLT). If you haven't done it yet, go ahead and "knock on Jesus' door" right now. It's as easy as saying:

Here I am, God. If you're real, then I want to know you. Please open my spiritual eyes so I can see you, and my spiritual ears so I can hear you. I'm asking you to forgive me for anything I've done that has come between us. And please come into my heart and make my life overflow.

Even as you are knocking on his door, Jesus has been knocking on yours as well. Because for Jesus, it's not just about you pursuing him or him pursuing you, he's genuinely interested in a two-way friendship with you…

"Look!" Jesus says, "I stand at the door and knock. If you hear my voice and open the door, I will come in, and we will share a meal together as *friends*" (REVELATION 3:20, emphasis added).

If you've ever had a conversation with Jesus—just now or at some point in your life—he's already gone to work inside you and is giving you new ways to see and hear him. Bend down the corner of this page and write today's date on the flap (or you can write the approximate date when you had a similar conversation with Jesus). If you aren't ready to begin a friendship with Jesus yet, bend down the flap anyway so you can find this page when you decide the time is right.

Getting to know Jesus is exciting stuff. Your heightened spiritual senses may take a while to develop (or re-energize), but if you've prayed for God to do this, you're on your way. As your spiritual senses begin to stir, you'll start to see things differently. You'll begin to experience God, his creation, and people around you in a whole new way. Fresh, unexpected thoughts will "pop" into your head. Steve calls these "flutter-bys"—fleeting, almost imperceptible whispers of God's still, small voice flickering through your head. You'll perceive them as whispers, not shouts, so it's easy to mistake them for your own thoughts. But as God continues honing your spiritual eyes and ears, you'll begin to tell the difference.

Loving, generous whispers—the ones that stretch you to go beyond what you would normally do—will stand out from everyday, self-focused thinking. The more God tunes your spiritual senses through Bible reading, Christian mentors, and time spent in prayer, the more you'll recognize the kinds of ideas that come from God and the kinds that don't. (Here's a clue: The condemning inner voices that call you a loser, tempt you to exploit others, or go against clear biblical teaching—those aren't coming from God.)

Getting to Know Jesus

As we said earlier, getting to know Jesus personally is very similar to getting to know any average mortal. For instance, if you want to become friends with anyone, it's a good idea to **get to know that person's story.**

You want to find out a little bit about where that person grew up and what experiences that person's had—like Steve's experiences as a student and then a pastor in Norway, or Dave's early life growing up in a military family and moving from coast to coast. Simple things like this tell you a lot about a person. And in Jesus' case, you can get to know his story by reading the first four books of the New Testament: Matthew, Mark, Luke, and John. By reading these books, you'll start learning Jesus' story and you'll find out more and more about Jesus' personality and motivations. You'll **get to know what Jesus likes and dislikes.**

Understanding how Jesus spent his time and the people he hung out with while he was on earth will tell you a lot about him. By reading the Bible, you'll find out what made Jesus laugh and cry, what excited him, and what made him angry. It's all right there in four short books.

Of course, even though you can learn a great deal from reading, you can never fully get to know someone from just reading a book. After all, there are fans who know everything there is to know about their favorite movie stars—their hometowns, what they eat for breakfast, who they're dating right now—but that doesn't mean they have two-way, personal friendships with them. They may know a lot *about* movie stars, but they don't *know* them. Fans might be able to relate to movie stars based on their perceptions, but that is not the same as having true relationships with them.

How can you tell if people *really* know and care about each other in a mutual way? Well, it may seem kind of obvious, but **they usually recognize one another.** They both know the sound of the other's voice, the way their friend's handwriting looks, and they can pick each other out in a crowd of strangers. According to Matthew 10:30, the Lord knows you so intimately he has the very hairs of your head numbered. Not only can God pick you out of a crowd, God's been paying so much attention to you he knows exactly which hairs are still on your head and which ones migrated to your hairbrush this morning!

Since you're only human, it takes time for you to get to know anybody well. Forget about hair counting (which is really hard to do with an invisible friend anyway), and think about just **spending time together with God** as you would with another friend. Intentionally spending time with God is a bit like driving. It doesn't matter who you are, driving takes focus. If you're impatient or distracted you're likely to miss important road signs or even hurt yourself. Spending quality time with God means slowing down. And, just like driving, it will become a regular part of your daily life—something that will begin to feel more comfortable and familiar.

Dave likes sitting on his front porch and "dialing down." Reading the Bible for a few minutes helps him slow his racing mind and concentrate on the spiritual "flutter-bys" we talked about earlier. Steve can create space to "hang out" with Jesus anywhere he can listen to music on his iPod. Learning how to spend time with God is a very personal discovery. So giving you a "how-to" list could get in the way. If you've invited God to reveal himself to you and give you eyes to see and ears to hear him, then God will answer your prayer. Just take time to slow down, talk to God, and pay attention to what's going on inside you and around you.

If you don't yet feel confident in your ability to hear and see God moving in your life, the next four readings will help you go deeper by listening to God, loving God, sharing with God, and serving God.

getting your **feet wet**

Describe your relationship with God right now. Would you say you're more like a critic, a fan, an acquaintance, a friend, an intimate partner, or a lover? Spend some time describing your relationship with God in the space below.

....

....

....

....

....

....

the **reflection** pool

>> What is keeping you from moving closer to God?

>> How could you personally go deeper with God?

>> How might having a deeper, two-way friendship with God change your life?

> "You've seen a lot, but looked at nothing.
>
> You've heard everything, but listened to nothing.
>
> God intended, out of the goodness of his heart, to be lavish in his revelation.
>
> But this is a people battered and cowed, shut up in attics and closets,
>
> Victims licking their wounds, feeling ignored, abandoned."
>
> **ISAIAH 42:20-22**
> (*The Message*)

"The reason we have two ears and only one mouth
is that we may listen the more and talk the less."

—Zeno of Citium (Circa 300 B.C.)

READING 7

listening to a still, small voice

Many years ago a very troubled young woman named Rebecca joined a small group Dave's wife, Pam, was leading in their inner-city neighborhood. Although Rebecca was only in her mid-twenties, it was apparent that life had not been kind to her. Severe drug and alcohol abuse had aged her prematurely. Extreme self-neglect and overeating had packed an extra 175 pounds onto her 5-foot-5-inch frame. Worst of all, her face emitted such tremendous hostility and gloom that others instinctively avoided her.

Fortunately, although Pam is somewhat introverted, she's also a person who listens to God. And one day as Rebecca was complaining how nobody cared for her or her situation, Pam had a sense that God wanted her to speak up in a pretty audacious way. Acting on her impression, Pam asked what it would take for Rebecca to believe that God cared for her. Rebecca just shrugged and looked at the floor. But quiet, mild-mannered Pam wouldn't drop the subject. "What would it take for God to *prove* to you that he loves you?" she asked.

After nearly a full minute of silence, Rebecca replied that if God would give her money to get a knee surgery she needed, and get her car fixed, and then get her a new job, she might possibly believe he cared. "OK," said Pam, "So go ahead and ask him!" Rebecca hemmed and hawed, but eventually stumbled through a simple prayer asking God for all three of the things she'd just mentioned. Two weeks passed before Pam saw Rebecca again and, as you might imagine, Pam was extremely curious.

"How have things been going?" Pam asked.

"Terrible," she replied in typical Rebecca fashion. Undaunted by her negative response, Pam continued,

"I'm just curious…were you able to get the money for your knee operation?"

"Yeah," grunted Rebecca after a guilty pause. "I got a check for $3,000 from a former employer out of a retirement account I'd forgotten all about." She went on to say it was exactly the amount needed for her knee operation.

"Wow!" said Pam, "That's just what you prayed for! What about your car?"

Again, Rebecca shrugged and nonchalantly said, "One of the guys in my neighborhood came by and fixed it. He said he was a Christian and he wanted to show me God's love by doing it for free."

By now Pam was almost too excited to contain herself. "Any news on the job front?" Pam inquired.

Again, Rebecca looked very uncomfortable and said, "Yeah, out of the blue I just got offered a new construction job, and it pays a lot more than I've been making."

Shy, unassuming Pam was practically dancing for joy at this point, but poor Rebecca still seemed as miserable as ever.

Though each and every one of Rebecca's prayers had been answered in just two weeks—all in ways she couldn't explain otherwise—Rebecca *still* wasn't recognizing God's message of love. Isaiah 30:18 (NIV) says, "Yet the Lord longs to be gracious to you; he rises to show you compassion." But unless you are willing to work at it, it's surprisingly easy to miss even blatantly miraculous forms of divine communication.

As far as Rebecca was concerned, her life was still "terrible." The dark cloud of what she'd been saying to herself *on the inside* for so many years still hung there—completely eclipsing the love God was so passionately trying to communicate.

But this story does have a happy ending! After lots of love and sacrifice from Pam and many others, Rebecca's ears and eyes eventually began to open. Though she still struggles, now we see the black cloud much less frequently and it's no longer unusual to see Rebecca with a big smile on her face.

Maybe your life has been as difficult as Rebecca's and maybe not, but either way there are factors that can get in the way of what God wants to communicate to you…and the blessings God wants to give you. Let's take a brief look at two of the biggies: the hurry factor and the worry factor.

The Hurry Factor

A deadline at work. Grocery shopping. An argument with a friend. An illness in the family…

Life is full.

Beyond basic unbelief, probably the most common reason people miss God is because they're distracted by too many other things. Pastor John Ortberg calls this tendency *Spiritual Attention Deficit Disorder.* In an age of rapid communication, we're also receiving an ever-growing volume of spiritual messages every day. Some are positive, but many come from the Thief we talked about in earlier chapters. As C.S. Lewis suggested in his classic book *The Screwtape Letters,* one of the Thief's favorite tactics is to distract our focus away from our relationship with God—and from anything important that God wants us thinking about—and get us thinking about lots of other things instead. That way we'll continue rolling down the gradual road to hell...or at least toward miserable ineffectiveness in our lives on earth.

There's an old saying that goes, "I always complained because my work was being interrupted—until I realized that *the interruptions were my work.*" There is a wonderfully counterintuitive truth here. Think back to Pam and Rebecca. Helping someone like Rebecca is something that most people who are in a hurry would almost never undertake—and would probably never want to. They'd look at Rebecca and all they'd see is a monster interruption to their already hectic schedules. As a matter of fact, before she met Pam a number of busy counselors, psychologists, and pastors had already written Rebecca off as "not worth their time." We can't say whether they were ignoring God's voice or not. All we know is that Pam, the guy who fixed Rebecca's car, and all the many others who slowed down long enough to show her kindness were acting with the kind of compassion Jesus showed toward the people he described as "confused and helpless, like sheep without a shepherd" (MATTHEW 9:36).

Have you ever heard the story of the woman who touched Jesus' cloak in Mark 5:24-34? Surrounded by a huge crowd, Jesus was hurrying to heal the dying daughter of a prominent leader. As Jesus quickly made his way through the crowds, a woman who'd suffered from 12 years of debilitating and untreatable bleeding reached out and touched him—and she was immediately healed. Even though Jesus' errand was truly a matter of life and death, he stopped to search out and talk with this woman.

Have you ever wondered why? If we had to hazard a guess, one reason is that—like Rebecca—this woman had come to believe she was low on God's priority list. She was sure Jesus had more important things to do than "waste his time" on her. Even so, she reached out and her little act of faith released the power of love. Her body was healed instantly, but for her spirit to be made whole, she needed to *hear* Jesus acknowledge her personally. She needed to *see* that to him she wasn't just an anonymous face in the crowd. And Jesus knew that. Jesus knew that to heal her spirit, he needed to communicate that she was worth his notice and *far more important than his busy schedule or the expectations of the crowd.*

Appeasing expectations that clamor for you to live at light-speed as you check off boxes on an impossible to-do list will all too easily distract you from noticing what's most important to God. Like the woman in Mark 5:24, you need to slow down and connect with Jesus—and let him connect with you.

We hope you aren't feeling guilty or anxious about your hurried life-style—that's neither our goal nor God's. On the contrary, our desire is just the opposite. We believe God wants you to feel peaceful and patient enough that you will scramble around *less* and accomplish *more* of what's *really* important in your life. If you think it's impossible, you'd be right. If not for divine inter-vention we'd all be lost beyond hope. Yet, as Jesus said in Matthew 19:26, "Humanly speaking, it is impossible. But with God everything is possible."

With God it's possible to prioritize relationship time. It's possible to get all your work done in 40 hours. It's possible to exercise, feed the kids, run errands…and still have time to invite someone like Rebecca for a cup of cof-fee or tea. It really is possible, but you have to trust God and trust that he can make it happen. Through God's power—and not your own—you can start to feel *less* guilty and hurried and stressed. You can actually feel like you have *more* time and are getting *more* done—both the things that you "have to do" and the things that you "want to do."

If hurrying is a big part of your life—and one of the biggest reasons you don't hear God—try saying words like these occasionally to God throughout the day:

> *God, right now my life is too busy. Help me find creative ways to slow down and live at a pace where I can hear and see you better. Help me to read the Bible and live so much like Jesus that I'll have eyes to see and ears to hear what you want to say to me.*

If you pray this way, and pay attention, we believe you'll experience some significantly amazing results. On the other hand, if you try to maintain the same ungodly pace as some of the people around you, don't be surprised if you miss incredibly rich answers to prayer pouring through your life—and, like Rebecca, see various aspects of your life as "terrible." After all, the words *terrible* and *hurry* just go together.

The Worry Factor

"The seed that fell among the thorns represents those who hear God's word, but all too quickly the message is crowded out by the worries of this life and the lure of wealth, so no fruit is produced" (MATTHEW 13:22).

Worry is another big reason we don't hear God's voice—we let our concerns drown him out. Worriers spend much of their time being driven here and there by fear that God is not really generous, or that he might not really show up when they need him most. Worriers try to take control of their own lives because they're afraid if they let go, everything will fall apart.

Worrying is a lack of trust.

It's a lack of trust that God is big enough or loving enough to care for your problems. It's a lack of trust that God's way is the best way. It's a fear that if you do it God's way instead of the world's way, then you'll lose out on something. It's a lack of trust that God knows you well enough to know what's best for your life. It's this fear that if you leave your life up to God you'll be disappointed in the outcome.

But God told the prophet Jeremiah, "I knew you before I formed you in your mother's womb. Before you were born I set you apart and appointed you as my prophet to the nations" (JEREMIAH 1:5). God *created* you for a purpose. God alone knows what you were created to do and what will best suit your personality and your desires. There's no reason to fear that God will give you a life you don't want, because when you're following God's plan for your life, you're living the life God created you to live. And that's when you'll be the most satisfied—the most fulfilled.

Dave tells his story—a story of when he almost gave in to the worries of this life and the lure of wealth.

> Twenty-seven years ago, when I was still young and single, I landed a remarkably high-paying job teaching high school far away from my family and friends. It was a great job, and I was making more than ever. There was only one problem: I started to dry up spiritually. It was the first time I'd been away from my tightknit community of Christian friends and, although I'd been a committed Christian for years, I found myself less and less inclined to pray or get up on Sunday morning to visit another church where I didn't feel like I fit in.

On the flip side, I was more and more inclined to slide into the temptations many young men are prone to. I knew better, and I was always regretful afterward, but it wasn't long before even that began to fade.

I'd forgotten the richness and joy of having a relationship with God. It had been clouded over with worries about money, things, and success. I'd swapped my first love for a lesser love—one that never left me satisfied.

Lucky for me, one of my best friends came for a visit. He sat down, looked around, and listened patiently as I told him how great my life was. When I stopped for air, he smiled at me and said, "Dave, you're trying pretty hard to sell me on how happy you are, but you look miserable to me. When the school year is over, why don't you come back home?"

I was shocked—couldn't he see how great I had it! I tried to argue, but then the truth hit me. I wasn't happy. I wasn't satisfied. I hadn't been for months. I missed my friends...and my God. I missed being filled with a greater joy and a greater purpose.

After the school year, I locked up my office and left for good. Sure, it was hard to give up the money and the lifestyle that went with it, but it wasn't long before I'd completely forgotten about it. I was satisfied again—filled to overflowing with love—from my friends and from God.

Even with no job, no place to stay, and a big car payment hanging over my head, it was like a giant weight had been lifted from my shoulders. And God gave me another job—one I enjoyed even more than the last one. And I found a place to live. I paid my bills. God took care of me—I'm not sure why I thought he wouldn't.

The truth is if I hadn't learned that lesson, I probably never would've overcome the worldly temptations of worry. I never would've gone into ministry. I never would've met the love of my life, and you would certainly not be reading this book. It was *a near thing*; I could have let the power of a few thousand bucks a month steal the rich future God had in mind for me. But because I learned to listen to God instead of my worries, I now have a life I never could have imagined in my teaching days. God is good!

When you're worried, it's often hard to believe that God wants to pour goodness and blessing through your life. Though there have been plenty of things to worry about, Dave has never regretted the decisions he made to trust God and to listen to him. In fact, what he's experienced has deepened Dave's faith and his trust because God has always followed through and taken care of the worries in Dave's life.

The Holy Spirit

In our experience, it's in the midst of slowing down and releasing your worries that you can most clearly hear God. Hurrying and worrying keeps you focused on yourself: the things *you* have to do, the problems *you* have to solve. But when you step out of your normal self-focused pattern—and begin to focus on what *God* wants you to do with your time and your thoughts—that's when you hear the Holy Spirit speaking in your life. In John 14:26, Jesus said his Father would send the Holy Spirit to all who follow Jesus to teach them all things and remind them of everything Jesus said in the Scriptures.

More often than not, when you slow down and listen to the Holy Spirit speak, the Spirit will remind you of something from the Bible—something Jesus said or did, something from Old Testament wisdom, or something insightful from the Epistles. The Holy Spirit will bring these things to mind at pertinent moments so that you can follow Jesus' example and grow to be more like him.

When Dave first began trying to listen to the Spirit, he half-expected God to tell him what clothes to wear and whether to turn right or left as he walked down the street. But that never worked.

"I was frustrated until I realized that God had already given me lots of specific guidance about the important things he wanted me to do. It wasn't 'turn right' or 'turn left' kind of stuff at all. It was 'Love your neighbor as yourself' (Matthew 22:39) and 'Be still, and know that I am God!' (Psalm 46:10). As I went out and tried do what *these* Scriptures commanded, I began to sense the Spirit prompting me and giving me more explicit instructions.

"I'm not always, absolutely, 100 percent sure these ideas are coming from God; but as long as they line up with the Bible and the love of Jesus, I can be pretty confident. As I've stepped out in this way, I've experienced

God's movement in thousands of ways—ways that could only otherwise be seen as 'mind-blowing coincidences.' The more I've risked and given my agenda over to God, the more I've grown in confidence that I really am recognizing the Spirit speaking in my heart."

It's just like with good friends: The more you engage in conversation and listen to one another, the closer you get. You learn everything there is to know about one another. You confide in one another during hard times. You get closer and closer as you share life together. It's the same with God. The more you listen to God, the closer you'll get to him, and the more you'll love him. And the more you love God, the more God's love will start to flow through you.

getting your feet wet

Sit down in a quiet place with very few distractions. Now stay there for 20 minutes. Listen.

What do you hear? Do you hear the clock ticking as you stress over the things you "should" be doing right now? Do you hear the nagging worries of today crowding out any peace of mind?

What is it that keeps you from being quiet in your heart and mind? from being still and knowing that God is, well, *God*—in control, and powerful enough to carry your burdens?

Pray now and ask God to still your heart, to make you aware of the things that steal your time, to help you give up control over your worries, and to trust him with your time and your problems.

> Then Jesus said, "Come to me, all of you who are weary and carry heavy burdens, and I will give you rest. Take my yoke upon you. Let me teach you, because I am humble and gentle at heart, and you will find rest for your souls. For my yoke is easy to bear, and the burden I give you is light" (MATTHEW 11:28-30).

....

....

....

....

....

....

....

....

the **reflection** *pool*

>> Pick a word that would describe how you feel most of the time (*stressed, behind, discouraged, concerned, afraid, calm, joyful, healthy*). Why does that word describe you? What word would you *like* to describe you?

>> How do you think listening to God can help you move from one word to the other?

>> How might listening to God change your relationships?

READING 8

loving the One who loved you first

A quick search of Amazon.com yields over 365,000 current books about love (imagine a stack of a thousand books for every day of the year); and there are over 100,000 books about God, Jesus, and the Holy Spirit. So if the amount written about a subject is any indicator of how much people are thinking about it, we probably think a lot more about love than we do about God. On the other hand, there are over five times as many books about God as there are about sex...there goes that theory.

So why are such a significant number of people writing books about love and God, or more to the point, why are so many people buying books about love and God? Maybe it's stating the obvious, but perhaps a great number of people aren't fully satisfied with their love lives *or* with their spiritual lives. It seems that almost everyone is hungry for deeper, richer, and more satisfying relationships. If our interactions with God or with others have been bad, we want better. If they've been good, we want even more.

So What Does It All Mean, Anyway?

Unfortunately, like so many of the words that Hollywood or Fifth Avenue has gotten hold of, *love* and *God* have been used and abused to the point where they might mean practically anything or virtually nothing depending on who's talking. And as we said, lots of people *are* talking and writing about them. Let's look at how *love* and *God* go together.

One common definition for love is *an intense feeling of deep affection*. Love can be the soaring romantic feeling that makes Prince Charming want to sing to Sleeping Beauty, or the unbearably tragic longing that moves the hideously deformed Quasimodo to risk his life and save the beautiful Esmeralda. Love is a little bit crazy. It causes people to take risks and make sacrifices for no other reason than to please or benefit their beloved. Infatuation and obsession can be self-focused and demanding. But *true love* isn't only passionate and enduring, it unfailingly puts the best interests of the beloved ahead of its own.

Contrary to prevailing images from television and movies, the love most of us hunger for is more than a feeling we fall into when the chemistry is right…or fall out of when things get too hard or confining. Love may begin with the gooey-eyed giving and receiving of valentines, but it only finds fulfillment in the faithful keeping of difficult vows. It's for richer *and* for poorer. It's in sickness *and* in health. It's about forsaking all others *and* signing up for joint savings and checking accounts. Real love is joyful *and* painful. It is extraordinary moments of rapture *and* everyday chores like washing dishes in the sink or picking your socks up off the floor. It's incredibly easy *and* totally impossible. Hundreds of thousands of books can't adequately express it, but somehow it's all there in the three simple words: "I love you!"

Interestingly, when the Apostle John looked for just the right words to explain what a relationship with God looks like, he used three simple words as well, "God is love" (1 JOHN 4:8b). John writes that if you don't love, you can't know God, because that's what his infinite power and unspeakable glory is in a nutshell—love. The greatest and most unselfish expression of love that has ever been seen on the planet was a message from God to you. Jesus' 30-year journey from the manger to the cross was all about demonstrating those three simple words to you. As John eloquently records:

"This is how much God loved the world: He gave his Son, his one and only Son. And this is why: so that no one need be destroyed; by believing in him, anyone can have a whole and lasting life" (JOHN 3:16, *The Message*).

Here is a compassion that transcends human failings. Here is a caring that lasts forever. It's a deeper, more real love that—unlike even the best parent or truest husband or wife—keeps each and every one of its promises. The popular word for this miracle is "unconditional love."

So what is our response to that?

How Can We Love God?

First John 4:19 says, "We love because he first loved us" (NIV). In other words, our love is a natural response to God's nearly incomprehensible kindness, passion, and sacrifice for us. Like a verse of the old hymn "How Great Thou Art": "When I think that God, his Son not sparing, sent him to die; I scarce can take it in."

"Taking in" the magnitude of God's gifts to us and grasping what they mean is part of what life is all about. In fact, a human lifetime isn't long enough to really "get it." That's why heaven was invented.

We've said that getting to know God has a lot in common with getting to know a friend. The same thing is true when it comes to loving God. When you really love someone, one of the things you almost unconsciously do is figure out what pleases that person. Watch the eyes of a couple in the first throes of young love. Watch how they intensely scan each other's faces for the slightest hint of pleasure. Without thinking about it, they tune in to the messages transmitted by tiny shifts in posture and minute movements in the eyes or mouth of their beloved. The only reward they're looking for is a big smile, a slight squeeze of the hand—any acknowledgement of the love they share.

This is listening *and then some*. The Bible paints a wonderfully similar picture when it says, "The Lord your God is with you...He will take great delight in you, he will quiet you with his love, he will rejoice over you with singing" (ZEPHANIAH 3:17, NIV).

But how can you return such love when you can't see the expression in God's eyes, or what makes his face light up? It actually is possible to find out what pleases God! God's given us an entire history to reveal what he loves and hates. Just look carefully at the stories in the Bible—the lives of the prophets, saints, apostles, and Jesus. Study the way they walked and talked with God.

Look at their acts of compassion toward hurting and hungry people—the honesty and respect they showed in talking to their heavenly Father. Indeed, by looking at the tiniest things Jesus and these others said and did on earth, you can know what makes God beam with joy.

Of course if you want a short list of the qualities that delight God's heart, just take a look at 1 Corinthians 13:4-8a:

"Love is patient, love is kind. It does not envy, it does not boast, it is not proud. It is not rude, it is not self-seeking, it is not easily angered, it keeps no record of wrongs. Love does not delight in evil but rejoices with the truth. It always protects, always trusts, always hopes, always perseveres. Love never fails" (NIV).

That's the amazing and challenging picture of God's love! It's exactly what we want from him and precisely what God longs for from us—both in our relationship with him and our relationships with everyone else. It's a pretty tall order unless we allow his love to get inside us and conquer our self-absorbed nature.

Steve finds great encouragement in the fact that Jesus is not only the miraculous Son of God, but over 60 times in the New Testament Jesus calls himself the "Son of Man."

"The idea is that it's not just the supernatural Son of God who can love like this. I think one reason Jesus called himself 'the Son of Man' so often was he wanted to make his kind of love available to human beings—and not just as recipients. No matter who we are, we can love like the Son of Man! His love flowing into us and through us provides *an anointing of credibility* to a world that is sick of falseness and 'fakey-anity.' Mother Teresa was only 4 feet 11 inches tall, but the authority that came from really loving people like Jesus made her a giant!"

Maybe you don't feel like you're in the same league as Mother Teresa, but if you act upon Christ's teachings and follow his example, God's love will truly be made complete in you (1 JOHN 2:5a, NIV). You will become living, breathing examples of God's love. First John 2:5-6 goes on to say that, "This is how we know we are in him: Whoever claims to live in him must walk as Jesus did" (NIV). You don't have to walk on water to walk like Jesus, but follow his example in the way you live each moment of your life. The secret isn't having miraculous powers at all; it's in allowing your love for God to guide your steps—just as Jesus did. If you've ever loved another human being in a truly unselfish way, you have some idea of what we're talking about.

How Loving God Is Like Loving Anyone

Loving someone subtly changes how you think and act. Instead of thinking and acting only for yourself, you begin plotting ways to show your love—saving up for gifts to give that person, secretly planning to take your loved one out to the perfect play, or trying to score tickets to the sold-out sporting event of a favorite team. Maybe when you go on a trip, you pick up little trinkets that say, "Even though we couldn't be together, I was thinking of you." Or maybe you pack little notes or surprises in his or her lunchbox or luggage. You may even go on a diet or sit (uncomplaining) through a movie or opera you can't stand. You make much bigger sacrifices because you know it will make that person happy. It may sound a little mushy, but loving God is kind of like that.

The same kinds of unselfish impulses apply to loving God. Instead of thinking of yourself, think about what you can do that will warm God's heart throughout the day. You know how much God loves generosity, so you go out of your way to do something kind in his name. Put change in the coin return of a pay phone wrapped in a note that says, "This is a free gift for you because God loves you!" You know how much God loves compassion, so call someone who is struggling and say, "God brought you to my mind today." Then invite that person to lunch and let him or her talk while you listen and show encouragement with your presence. You know how much God loves spending time alone with you, so set aside an hour to just have a long conversation with God—no particular agenda in mind, just a time to share your thoughts and listen.

Though God knows everything and never leaves your side, God still enjoys it when you joyfully do things *just because* you know God likes them. That's part of what 2 Corinthians 9:7 means when it says, "God loves a person who gives cheerfully." Though love and duty invariably go hand in hand, God wants you to experience joy in being loved by him and in loving him back. You wouldn't feel dutifully obliged to go out and get those tickets for the special sporting event or the play we talked about earlier…you'd just naturally do it to please the one you love. And you'd be excited about doing it. That's exactly how it can be with God—a natural and overwhelming desire to make God happy. The more you love God, the more excited you'll be about doing things with God and for God.

There is a word to describe putting your devotion for God into words and actions. The word is *worship*. It's another one of those words that has lost some of its power and meaning over the last few centuries. Our word for worship comes from the Old English *weorthscipe:* to regard with ardent or adoring esteem or devotion...to show God's true worth by your words and your deeds.

Unfortunately many people today think of worship as synonymous with religious ceremonies that involve singing—ceremonies that primarily take place in churches on Sunday mornings. It's simply not true...this is such a limited version of a concept that is meant to be very rich and personal. The Bible describes a much more holistic idea of worship: "Take your everyday, ordinary life—your sleeping, eating, going-to-work, and walking-around life—and place it before God as an offering. Embracing what God does for you is the best thing you can do for him" (ROMANS 12:1, *The Message*).

This is a picture of worship that can happen any place or any time. If you like to sing, sing to God about what he means to you. If you like to go hiking, take a hike and talk with God. Stop every now and then to breathe in the fresh air and appreciate the beauty around you—the beauty God made. If you like to write, write him a poem or an essay. If you like to build with your hands, make something for God and give it to somebody he'd want to have it. You get the picture. Whatever it takes for you to live everyday moments in a way that expresses God's wonder and worth—that's what worship is. Going to church is a good thing. We highly recommend finding a congregation where people really want to experience and show love for God; sharing your joy with others just makes it richer. But please don't confine your worship to the inside of any building. It's just not natural.

Loving and worshipping God is all-inclusive. It involves setting aside time to talk and to listen. It involves reading and studying the stories of Scripture and continuing that story in your own life. It involves discovering the gifts and talents God has given you, and using those talents to bring joy to God. This is the worship God wants—and it's probably more exciting than you ever imagined. As your love grows, so will the depth and variety of ways you can connect with God.

It's very possible to love someone who is invisible in such a way as to make that someone become visible to the eyes of your heart. We can live as Peter, one of Jesus' closest followers, encourages us to do:

"Though you have not seen him, you love him; and even though you do not see him now, you believe in him and are filled with an inexpressible and glorious joy" (1 Peter 1:8, NIV). If you're still not quite sure what developing and sharing deeper, more intimate connections with God might look like for *you*; well, that's the topic of the next reading.

getting your **feet wet**

Set aside an hour and plan something really special to do with or for God. Maybe you can do something we described in this chapter, such as a hike with God, time spent showing compassion to those who are hurting, or an hour of journaling your thoughts to God. Or maybe you have your own ideas of how to "surprise" God with your love for him.

the **reflection** *pool*

>> Did anything in this chapter surprise or impact you? Why?

>> How might the idea of personal, everyday worship change the way you live your life?

>> When do you feel like it's easiest for you to show God love? How can you show God love during other times throughout your day?

"Make sure you don't take things for granted and go slack in working for the common good; share what you have with others. God takes particular pleasure in acts of worship—a different kind of "sacrifice"—that take place in kitchen and workplace and on the streets."

—HEBREWS 13:16
(*The Message*)

"Infinite sharing is the law of God's inner life."

—Thomas Merton,
No Man Is an Island (1955)

READING 9

sharing it all with God

What can you possibly share with God? After all, he literally *does* have everything.

It's just a silly story, of course, but what comes to mind is the children's Christmas book *The Littlest Angel.* Maybe you heard this story as a child, or maybe you've read it to your own kids. As its title implies, it's a story about the youngest angel in heaven who was "exactly four years, six months, five days, seven hours and forty-two minutes of age" when he showed up at the pearly gates. From his first day forward—though heaven was majestic and full of beauty—this little guy just didn't fit in very well. And as time went by, he was more and more miserable.

Eventually a kind, elder angel realized that this little angel's sadness was really homesickness—for his life as a little boy back on earth. Everything changed for the better once the little angel was allowed to retrieve a small, rough, unsightly little box from under his bed "back home." The box contained the kinds of treasures little boys often collect: a butterfly with golden wings, a sky-blue egg from a bird's nest, two white stones from a muddy river bank, and a tooth-marked leather strap once worn as a collar by his pet dog. But to the littlest angel, these homely little objects were a secret source of delight. When the time came for Jesus to be born on earth, all the angels of heaven brought gifts and placed them before the throne of God. Our little angel buddy laid down his precious box, even though he worried what God would think of his humble offering.

Dave says,

"For some reason, though I'm over 50 years old and not a particularly emotional guy, I can't ever get through this story without getting choked up. I actually have to hold back tears every time I read the part where God says, 'Of all the gifts of all the angels, I find that this small box pleases me most.' In fact, it was so special that the story says God transformed that lowly box into the Star of Bethlehem—a beacon to all who would bring their gifts to honor Jesus.

"When I think about it, I guess there is something deep inside me—and perhaps deep inside everybody—that wants God to treasure the humble things that we love most. Though you and I may think we're nothing special and don't have much to give, God disagrees. For reasons the angels don't even fully understand, he values us and our humble little offerings of time, talents, and money far beyond mountains or oceans of gold and anything else we might think of."

It's a nice story—but it's still just a story. The author made it all up complete with "nursery-appropriate" pictures of angels and how things work up in heaven. And yet this fictional story holds biblical truths many of us grown-ups have forgotten all about.

A Little Mustard Seed and a Bit of Yeast

Jesus used two illustrations, one right after the other. First, he said, "The Kingdom of Heaven is like a mustard seed planted in a field. It is the smallest of all seeds, but it becomes the largest of garden plants; it grows into a tree, and birds come and make nests in its branches." Then Jesus continued, "The Kingdom of Heaven is like the yeast a woman used in making bread. Even though she put only a little yeast in three measures of flour, it permeated every part of the dough" (MATTHEW 13:31-33).

Both of these similes are meant to illustrate how little things—things we're tempted to discount and ignore—can make a bigger difference than we first imagined. A single mustard seed is nothing to look at. It's smaller than a grain of sand, but if you plant it in your field, it can grow to over 10 feet in height.

Maybe you've picked up on it already, but one of Steve's great heroes is Mother Teresa. As we mentioned earlier, she was a little woman, standing at just 4 feet 11 inches tall. But she was only "little" on the outside—the same way a mustard seed is little. On the inside—where her relationship with God was growing—were all the gigantic makings of a world-changer. Nobody understood when, relatively late in her life and with very little support from her religious order, she set out for Calcutta. But she didn't care what anyone else thought; she believed she was called to work with poor Indian people who were dying in the streets.

When she got to Calcutta, leaders of the religious charities and government agencies tried to discourage her. They said they were already doing all that could be done for the city's poor. Undaunted, this "little" woman began physically carrying dying beggars off the street and into a tiny hospice. She did everything she could think of to tend the beggars' wounds and show them the love of Jesus during the last few days, hours, and minutes of their earthly lives. The story goes that near the end of Mother Teresa's life, a journalist asked her how many of these poor souls she'd carried off the streets and she guessed somewhere between 30,000 and 35,000. Shocked, he asked, "How did you ever help so many?" The answer she gave was a little unexpected. "If I hadn't carried the first one," she said, "I couldn't have carried the 30,000th."

In other words, before that little mustard seed can grow to tower over the rest of the garden plants, it must be planted. If it sits in its safe little packet with all the other seeds, no shoots will ever spring up to seek the sunlight, and no roots will ever go down into the soil to draw nourishment or support the growing plant. It will just grow stale on the shelf. The same is true for yeast—the tiny living fungus that ferments the sugar in bread dough and causes it to rise. A minute bit of yeast can infect a huge vat of dough in the most positive way possible, enriching it and increasing it in size 50 percent 100 percent or even 1000 percent. But in order to do its job, that yeast must be put into the dough. For Mother Teresa to become the world-changer God created her to be, she had to first leave her safe home and make the journey to Calcutta. She had to pick up that first beggar and tend to his wounds.

As anyone who has ever spent time in a bakery or a kitchen knows, yeast not only causes bread to rise, it infects the very atmosphere around it with its wholesome aroma. This echoes the Scripture that says when we follow Jesus, we bring "the aroma of Christ" to those around us (2 CORINTHIANS 2:15, NIV). This aroma doesn't come from grand gestures or even our tremendous talent. It comes from lots of tiny, no-big-deal atoms of goodness we've shared with God and allowed him to use for his purposes.

Of the many profound things Mother Teresa said during her lifetime, one quote in particular captures this thought. She said, "Not everyone can do great things, but everyone can do small things with great love." Steve has transformed those words into a battle cry for ordinary people who want their lives to make an extraordinary difference in the world. His version goes like this: "Small things done with great love will change the world!"

What we've been taught all our lives (especially us Americans) is that big celebrities with big bank accounts are the ones who change the world—but that's just not true! Anyone—*anyone*—who is motivated by God's love can change the world. Anyone—*anyone*—who is willing to leave the safety of everyday routine for the sake of saving lives (physical and eternal), can change the world.

That's the mustard-seed mindset: Letting God plant you in the world so you can become a towering tree—one that represents faith, love, and the hope of God. That's the yeast way of life—acknowledging that those little, insignificant-seeming talents and opportunities God has placed in your hands can give rise to hope in the hearts of those around you. Just because your contributions might seem small, don't let that stop you from sharing them with God.

If this sounds a little cosmic, maybe the following story will bring it down to earth for you.

Start Small

A few years ago, Steve was invited to Kenya to speak in Eldoret, an area a couple hours north of Nairobi. About 1,000 people showed up for a two-day conference centered on living the generous, "outward-focused" life modeled by Jesus and the early church. After hearing hours of Bible teachings and practical examples of how Steve's church had practiced mustard-seed-sized actions in his community, the church's elders gathered. Steve describes what happened next:

> They huddled for about 30 minutes, and then came and told me, "We have decided that this is a biblical idea and it is something the Holy Spirit is calling us to take part in from now on. We will begin tomorrow with all of our people. What do you suggest we do that wouldn't cost a lot?"
>
> The first idea that popped into my head was cleaning up the trash that was piled up everywhere in the streets of Eldoret. So that's what I suggested to the elders, and that's what they announced to their people. "Tomorrow we will *all* come at 8:30 with buckets from home and then we will *all* go out and clean up our city to show Christ's love. See you all in the morning!"
>
> Based on my experiences with the American churches I'd worked with, I expected maybe a couple of dozen people to show up. But the next morning at 8:30, there were over 1,000 people gathered and ready with buckets in hand! There they were, from 4-year-old children to 90-year-old senior citizens, linking arms and sweeping through the streets of the city. Every speck of litter, every shard of broken glass, every piece of paper, every cigarette butt on the streets disappeared into their buckets!
>
> You could literally see where the kingdom of God had been and where it had yet to go just by looking at the ground. Where it was clean, Christ's followers had been there. Where it was covered with garbage, they hadn't gotten there yet.
>
> I don't know how it started, but soon our crowd of Christian street cleaners began singing beautiful, Swahili worship songs. To me, it was

nothing short of heavenly. And I wasn't the only one who saw it. Many passers-by stopped in their tracks to watch and listen. Some even began to weep at what they saw. A photojournalist from the Kenya Times who was passing by snapped many pictures of "the cleansing of Eldoret."

Like so many others, she asked: "Tell me, why are you people cleaning up trash?" Over and over, she got the same response: "If Jesus were in our city, he wouldn't just be preaching in a church, he'd be out sharing his love in practical ways. So we are out cleaning up trash in the same spirit."

The next day, a big article appeared on the front page of the national newspaper she worked for. The headline read, "Christians Share Love By Serving!" Even though everyone was talking about it, it was just a *little* thing. It was something so simple and so humble that anyone could do it. For a few hours, they just gave Jesus their hands so he could pick up garbage, and gave him their voices to announce his coming. And wherever they went, Jesus miraculously transformed their humble gift of an average Saturday morning into a beacon—like a little star of Bethlehem—pointing the way to the Savior.

How about you? You may not be able to travel to Kenya to preach, but you could clean up the trash in your neighborhood. You may not be able to pick up beggars off the streets of Calcutta, but you could visit a homeless shelter this weekend to serve and pray for those who are there. You may not be able to donate thousands of dollars to your favorite charity, but you could buy lunch for the person in line behind you at McDonald's.

You get the picture. It's small things done with great love. It's a willingness to share your life with God—for whatever purpose. It's a willingness to share your love with those that God loves—to whatever end.

Sharing the Details

Your time and talents are not the only things God wants to share with you. God desperately wants to share a friendship with you—an intimate, deep relationship.

Think of the things you share with your best friends: conversation, laughter, good times and bad times...

It's what God wants with you, too. More than anything else, God wants you to share the details of your life with him. God wants you to tell him when and why you're happy; God wants you to share with him the desires of your heart, your hopes for the future, and your joys in the present.

And God wants you to share with him your burdens: your fears, worries, doubts, and struggles. Psalm 55:22 urges you to cast all your cares on God so he can sustain you and hold you up.

You might be poor, depressed, confused, captive to an addiction, or just in need of a little encouragement. Whatever is going on with you, God wants you to share it with him so that he can help you bear it and overcome it. Pouring out your heart to God gives you a confidant and more—it allows you to transfer your worries and hurts into God's safekeeping. It helps quiet your fears and make room for God's Holy Spirit to flow in and become your comforter.

The overflowing life is all about giving to God and receiving from him. These two things are eternally and inextricably linked. If all you do is give and give and give and never receive, soon you'll be empty and worn out. Though it may start out as generosity, when you give and never receive, your giving becomes *all about you*. It becomes condescending, prideful, and ultimately arrogant. The love in it dies and shrivels into grudging obligation. It becomes a selfish martyrdom that's more about everything *you've* sacrificed than it is about the people you're helping. It's ugly and it's not what God desires.

As we've said over and over, God wants to fill you to overflowing with his love—and then you will always have more than enough to sincerely and gladly share with him and others.

Second Corinthians 9:8 says, "God is able to make *all grace* abound to you, so that in *all things* at *all times*, having *all that you need*, you will abound in *every good work*" (NIV, emphasis added). There's a promise! When this verse says *all grace* it's talking about the limitless, overflowing favor and blessings God wants to give you because he loves you. Since it's a gift, you don't have to earn it by doing good works. But you do have to constantly open up space in your heart to receive *all the things* you need in *all the times* when you need them.

This means having an active, nonstop conversation with God like the one

Jesus carried on with his Father throughout the Gospels. This is what 1 Thessalonians 5:17 means when it tells us to "pray without ceasing" (KJV). A life *abounding* in every good work is the natural result. As 2 Corinthians 9:10-11, says, "For God is the one who provides seed for the farmer and then bread to eat. In the same way, he will provide and increase your resources and then produce a great harvest of generosity in you.

Yes, *you will be enriched in every way so that you can always be generous.* And when we take your gifts to those who need them, *they will thank God*" (emphasis added).

Whatever you've got to share—be it talent, time, treasures, or just the troubles you're worrying about right now—place it in God's hands and it will be miraculously transformed into something that can change the world.

getting your **feet wet**

Find three things in your house that represent three areas of interest for you. For example, you might choose a basketball because you play with your buddies every Tuesday, or you might choose a family photo to represent the importance you place on them.

Once you have your three items, pray and ask God how you can share each of those areas of interest with him. Maybe you could invite someone new to play basketball each week? Or maybe you and your family could devote one Saturday a month to neighborhood service?

Write your thoughts in the space below.

....

....

....

....

....

....

....

....

....

....

....

....

....

the reflection pool

>> What do you find easiest to share with God? most difficult? Why do you think that is?

>> In the past, what's happened when you chose to share something with God?

>> What daily steps could you take to share more of your life with God?

> "Serve wholeheartedly,
> as if you were serving the
> Lord, not men, because
> you know that the Lord
> will reward everyone for
> whatever good he does…"
>
> —EPHESIANS 6:7-8A (NIV)

> "I know God will not give
> me anything I can't handle.
>
> I just wish that he didn't
> trust me so much."
>
> —Mother Teresa

READING 10

serving God with love

Before the war, they were playing sandlot baseball in Brooklyn, working in the family grocery store in Illinois, running a traveling blacksmith shop in Texas, and then suddenly—in a day—everything changed. Pearl Harbor was attacked, and some enlisted immediately while others got caught up in the draft that followed. Others traded in their housekeeping duties for grueling factory work.

These days we know them as "the greatest generation." But what is it that made them so great?

The simple answer is: *They all became servants in a cause that was greater than their own lives.* Though many, no doubt, complained at the hardship and were scared to death by what they were asked to do, *they did it anyway*. As far as they were concerned, the world was in trouble and somebody had to do something. Like it or not, they were called. What makes so many of our fathers, mothers, grandfathers, and grandmothers so great is that they showed up and did what had to be done. They pulled together to face unbeatable odds and—through solidarity, sacrifice, and struggle—they beat those odds. Whatever your political persuasion, it's hard not to admire their willingness to step up and serve—especially when you consider that most of them will say they did it for us.

A Hidden Treasure

Jesus said, "The Kingdom of Heaven is like a treasure that a man discovered hidden in a field. In his excitement, he hid it again and sold everything he owned to get enough money to buy the field" (MATTHEW 13:44).

Though it may sound a little odd to the ears of modern readers, the New Testament Greek word translated as "treasure" in this verse is *thēsauros*, like *Roget's Thesaurus*. That big fat book on your shelf is called a thesaurus because it's a *treasure house of words.* Maybe it doesn't seem particularly relevant, but we're going through all this etymology to help you realize that the treasure hidden in the farmer's field wasn't a precious coin or even a big pirate chest filled with precious coins—it was a lot more significant than that. Dave likes to imagine it as something similar to the huge, subterranean treasury shown in the movie *National Treasure.* If you haven't seen it, this 2004 film shows nearly endless galleries heaped so full of gold, jewels, and priceless artwork that it would make the richest Pharaoh drool with excitement.

So what does the man do? That's right, he carefully hides the secret entrance to the amazing storehouse he's discovered. Then as quickly and quietly as possible, he sells his house, horse, plow, and everything else he can think of in order to buy that field—the whole time knowing he's getting the best bargain in the history of the world! After all, what's an old house, or an old plow, or anything he ever dreamed of having compared to the secret he's stumbled on?

That's what the kingdom of heaven is like! The question is, what are we willing to let go of in order to become spiritual gazillionaires? Jesus doesn't pretend there's no cost or that it won't be difficult to sell all we have. In fact, he paints a very graphic picture saying, "If any of you wants to be my follower, you must turn from your selfish ways, take up your cross daily, and follow me.

If you try to hang on to your life, you will lose it. But if you give up your life for my sake, you will save it" (LUKE 9:23-24). In other words: You can have more than you ever dreamed and all it will cost is following me in my sacrifice. But the joy ahead of you will make the sacrifice worth it. To use the words of the famous missionary and martyr Jim Elliot, "He is no fool who gives what he cannot keep to gain what he cannot lose."

We want to serve God both as a loving response to all he's given to us and because we've glimpsed the staggering richness that comes from being with him in this world and the next. As 1 John 4:19 says, "We love because he first loved us" (NIV). We don't serve in order to be accepted; we serve *because* we are accepted—it's a natural *outflowing* of our relationship with God. God loves us whether we serve or not, but our relationship with him—our treasure—is so much richer if we serve him. It's just one more layer of our relationship—one more aspect that makes our intimacy deeper. We listen to God. We love God. We share with God. We serve God. None of those alone is the key to a perfect relationship. And when any one is missing, then the relationship will be lacking. The treasure is not complete. But, together, they create an intimacy and a unity that is beyond any earthly fortune.

God doesn't demand that you serve in order to earn his love, but God wants you to serve in order to experience the joys of a more complete relationship. Just as the relationship with your friends or spouse is enriched when you serve one another, so it is with God. And the closer you get to God, the more you'll desire to serve him. Perhaps this is why Jesus took some of his last few precious hours on earth to wash the feet of his disciples. Here's how the Apostle John described it:

"Jesus knew that the Father had given him authority over everything and that he had come from God and would return to God. So he got up from the table, took off his robe, wrapped a towel around his waist, and poured water into a basin. Then he began to wash the disciples' feet, drying them with the towel he had around him" (JOHN 13:3-6).

As we mentioned back in Chapter 5, in those status-conscious days foot washing was a task reserved for only the youngest and lowliest household servants. That's undoubtedly why Peter forcefully protests by saying, "No... you will never ever wash my feet!" (JOHN 13:8a). After all, Jesus was Peter's master, not some foot-washing flunky! But Jesus silenced him, saying,

"Unless I wash you, you won't belong to me" (JOHN 13:8b). Once Peter and the rest of the disciples experienced the shock of having their feet washed and dried by their master and Messiah, Jesus asks them, "Do you understand what I was doing?" (JOHN 13:12b). Imagine their stunned silence as he went on to explain his purpose in serving them: "You call me, 'Teacher' and 'Lord,' and you are right, because that's what I am. And since I, your Lord and Teacher, have washed your feet, you ought to wash each other's feet. I have given you an example to follow. Do as I have done to you" (JOHN 13:13-15).

Though it's popular these days to talk about servant leadership, Jesus wasn't just talking. He was a servant first and foremost. And Jesus was calling his disciples to take up their basins and towels and to follow him. Jesus' kingdom won't be like the ones we know so well—where the strongest, smartest, and most ruthless get what they want by focusing on their own ambitions. His would be a kingdom where love, faithfulness, and service would get you everywhere. Jesus described it, saying, "You know that the rulers in this world lord it over their people, and officials flaunt their authority over those under them. But among you it will be different. Whoever wants to be a leader among you must be your servant, and whoever wants to be first among you must become your slave. For even the Son of Man came not to be served but to serve others and to give his life as a ransom for many" (MATTHEW 20:25b-28).

Jesus concluded the foot-washing experience by telling his disciples, "Now that you know these things, God will *bless* you for doing them" (JOHN 13:17, emphasis added). Jesus was saying that if we humble ourselves and take on his servant lifestyle, he'll pour out even more of his favor on us and through us. And as we serve we'll experience power and favor from his inexhaustible love flowing through us.

Dave recently attended the funeral of an 84-year-old friend named Bob—a friend whom Dave had seen almost every single Tuesday for over a decade. Every week Bob would faithfully show up and volunteer to assemble training materials and help out around Dave's ministry office. Dave always looked forward to Tuesdays for Bob wasn't just a faithful volunteer, he was also a continuous source of encouragement and support to Dave and the ministry. Of course that's not where Bob's story begins...

Bob had been one of the officers present when the Japanese signed
the surrender at the end of World War II on board the battleship Mis-
souri. After that Bob had moved up the ranks of corporate America and
become a top executive in one of the nation's largest insurance com-
panies. Though those were great accomplishments, they weren't Bob's
greatest treasure. Bob's greatest treasure was his friendship with Jesus.
And Bob's greatest joy came from serving people in Christ's name.

Bob served his wife, Lillian, his family, and his church in thousands of
little ways. He secretly helped people in financial trouble so they could
get back on their feet again. Hundreds of children coming to Sunday
school all knew "Grandpa Bob." He'd been there rain or shine—as long
as they could remember—to give them a big hug on their way in the
doors. Children he'd greeted years before still stopped to get their hugs
as they dropped their own children off for Sunday school.

Serving wasn't a burden to Bob because it was an essential part of
a growing friendship with Jesus. He had struggles and problems like
everybody else, but the joyful Spirit of God was so present in Bob that
it went wherever he went. In serving, Bob had grown closer and closer
to God, and everyone around him rejoiced because of it.

A Pearl of Great Price

Jesus continued on with his description of the kingdom of heaven with a
second illustration. He said: "The Kingdom of Heaven is like a merchant on
the lookout for choice pearls. When he discovered a pearl of great value, he
sold everything he owned and bought it!" (MATTHEW 13:45-46). This pearl is
not just one-in-a-million. It's much more extraordinary than that. It's the
ultimate pearl— the only one of its kind. Until now the merchant has only
dreamed such a treasure might even exist. If the biblical merchant were a
modern fisherman, finding that pearl would be like hooking the legendary
"Big Red." Though the names may vary from location to location, we're talking
about the huge, crafty catfish thousands of fishermen have been dreaming of

and trying to catch all their lives. If you hang around many fishermen, you'll hear outrageous stories about a catfish that has lived for 50 years, 100 years, and...*gulp*, 150 years—a fish that has just kept growing and growing. They'll tell you about a catfish that's bigger than an NFL player. And once in a blue moon, somebody actually catches a fish like Big Red. Pictures of these fish— and the triumphant anglers who hauled them in—stagger the imaginations of veteran fishermen everywhere and make them hunger all the more to catch their local version of "Big Red."

You don't stumble across a wily old fish like "Big Red" or, for that matter, a prize pearl like Jesus is talking about. You have to seek it out and diligently pursue it morning, noon, and night. Jesus is quite clear that, unlike the man who *accidentally* came by the treasure house hidden in the field, the merchant was purposely focused on his job of finding fine pearls the day he found his once-in-a-lifetime pearl. The merchant didn't have to ponder, "Should I or shouldn't I go for it." As a wise and experienced merchant, he recognized immediately that this particular pearl was worth everything he had. He didn't hesitate; he didn't call his accountant to ask him what he could afford to invest. No—he rushed away and sold it all without even thinking twice.

Most of us have been trained to think that this kind of behavior is for reckless, irresponsible, crazy people. But Jesus was ushering in a new kind of kingdom with a different kind of mindset. In fact, we think the story Jesus is telling about the merchant who gave up everything he had for one pearl is *autobiographical*. He is the merchant and—though it's incredibly hard to take this in—*you* are his pearl of great price.

Let that sink in. Jesus knew exactly what he was doing when he bet everything he had on you. He did it with passion. He did it with joy. He did it with the wild hope that you would someday understand just how precious you are to him. Jesus wants you to know that he's the treasure house that's always been just underneath the fields where you've been toiling. Jesus has been longing to guide you through the entrance of his treasure trove and to open room after room overflowing with life like you've never imagined it. Like Dave's friend Bob, you can start experiencing this treasure right here on earth by walking with Jesus now.

The key to all of it is serving. Serving is what walking with Jesus is all about. Everything Jesus says and does is out of deep love for his Father and us. Read Jesus' words as he poured out his heart in the garden of Gethsemane, "My Father! If it is possible, let this cup of suffering be taken away from me. Yet I want your will to be done, not mine" (MATTHEW 26:39b). Instead of focusing on himself, Jesus served his Father, knowing it was the only way to bring you and all of us eternal life.

It's Not About Guilt!

We're not trying to guilt or bribe you into anything—true service flows from a loving relationship and not from a sense of obligation. Of course there will be many days when you don't feel like serving God or anybody else. We've all been there—and we'll talk about that a lot in upcoming chapters. We've looked at the sacrifices and service of friends like Bob from the World War II generation; we've seen how they changed the world with their bravery and love. In the next section we'll continue the outward journey with some courageous steps of our own. We'll learn to let our faith and love flow outward in ways that refresh and encourage our friends and family—and draw them closer to God.

getting your **feet wet**

Take a look at your calendar and pick out an evening or a morning this week that you could set aside for serving God in some way.

Block out a couple of hours. Then think of some little act of service that might bring a smile to God's face. It could be around your house or around your neighborhood. For example, you might give your spouse a foot massage, or you might go to a self-service gas station and offer to wash windows or pump gas for free.

If anyone asks what you're doing, just say you're trying to learn how to serve like Jesus.

the **reflection** *pool*

>> When you think of the rewards of a relationship with Jesus, what comes to mind?

>> What is your motivation for serving God—or people—right now? How might a shift in motives change the way you view service?

>> How can service lead to a closer relationship with God?

the **deep end**

A REFLECTION ON RELATIONSHIP

Your relationship with God is the key to *Outflow*. Without a growing, intimate friendship with God, none of the rest of this works. *Outflow* is meant to be a natural, everyday part of your life. Which means it has to originate and be driven by God's love flowing out of you, something that will only happen if your relationship with God is healthy and growing.

Use this Deep End experience to reflect on your friendship with God. Find a favorite spot where you enjoy sitting alone. Take a journal or a blank piece of paper, and spend some time reflecting on and writing about the current state of your relationship with God. Consider using the following prompts to guide your time with God:

• When do you most enjoy spending time with God? How do you usually spend that time?

• What words would you use to describe God? How has God embodied those words in your life?

• If you could choose one Scripture verse and one quote from outside of Scripture to describe your relationship with God, what would they be?

• How could you use a discipline, such as prayer, worship, fasting, or reading the Bible, to deepen your friendship with God? What might that look like in the days to come?

• How does God fill you? How can you overflow this into others?

If you're going through *Outflow* with a small group, summarize your thoughts from today's time with God, and send an e-mail to the other members of your group. Or consider setting aside part of your next small group time to discuss this Deep End experience.

group
discussion questions

Use these questions during your small-group time and dia-logue together about the second week of Outflow *readings.*

>> How could you personally go deeper with God? What actions could you take in the upcoming weeks to change your relationship with God?

>> Pick a word that would describe how you feel most of the time (for example: *stressed, behind, discour-aged, concerned, afraid, calm, joyful, healthy*). Why does that word describe you? What word would you *like* to describe you? How do you think listening to God can help you move from one word to the other?

>> What time of the day do you feel it's easiest for you to show God love? How can you show God love dur-ing other times of your day?

>> What is easiest for you to share with God? most dif-ficult? Why do you think that is?

>> What are your motives for serving God—or people—right now? How might a shift in motives change the way you view service?

OUTFLOW

you

your family
& friends

outward toward family and friends

READING 11

judea

How can something so simple and natural be so scary at the same time? For many of us, the very thought of talking about God with our family and friends is loaded with conflicting emotions. If you're growing in love and commitment to Jesus in the ways we've described in the previous section, part of you is probably already longing, as 1 Peter 3:15 puts it, to overflow "the hope that you have" into the next tier of your fountain: the people closest to you. On the other hand, you know your family and you know your friends well enough to recognize they're all in very different places, spiritually speaking. Some may be quite receptive and others much less so.

Flinging Seeds

We believe Jesus had your situation in mind as he spoke to a group of his followers along the shore of a lake.

"Listen! A farmer went out to plant some seeds. As he scattered them across his field, some seeds fell on a footpath, and the birds came and ate them. Other seeds fell on shallow soil with underlying rock. The seeds sprouted quickly because the soil was shallow. But the plants soon wilted under the hot sun, and since they didn't have deep roots, they died. Other seeds fell among thorns that grew up and choked out the tender plants. Still other seeds fell on fertile soil, and they produced a crop that was thirty, sixty, and even a hundred times as much as had been planted! Anyone with ears to hear should listen and understand" (Matthew 13:3b-9).

It almost goes without saying that Jesus was talking to people who were intimately acquainted with planting seeds. Though not all were farmers, most depended on what was growing in their family gardens as a vital part of their daily sustenance. For many years we've been trying to help modern Americans and Europeans—who've never planted or watered anything other than their front lawns—to think like first-century Hebrew gardeners. First off, back then they didn't just hop in their car and buzz down to the local garden center to pick up seeds. They collected the seeds from everything they harvested or ate so they could sow the seeds back into the soil for the next season. Though we spit out the seeds of oranges and watermelons or throw them in the trash without giving them a second thought; Hebrew gardeners always sowed their seeds back into the soil—knowing that today's seed is next year's crop.

As Jesus later explained, "The seed," he was referring to, "is God's Word" (Luke 8:11). The Greek word translated as *word* here is *logos*, and its etymology is fascinating. *Logos* means far more than a collection of characters written on a page or syllables spoken out loud. Those are things that can get garbled in translation. *Logos* means the *true essence* of what God is actually communicating. It's so significant that the Apostle John begins the fourth Gospel using the word three times in a row: "In the beginning was the Word, and the Word was with God, and the Word was God" (John 1:1, NIV).

God wasn't content to simply dictate a bunch of words to his prophets or write his laws on stone. In order to be absolutely, perfectly clear in transmitting his intentions toward you and the whole human race, he came in person to live a life of love and sacrifice. John 1:14 tells us, "the Word became flesh and made his dwelling among us" (NIV).

OK. Back to the seed-sowing parable. The big idea—the reason we just spent a bunch of time dissecting the history of one word—is that the seed we sow into the lives of others is *Jesus,* and Jesus' whole life was about love.

If we've chosen to have a relationship with Jesus and his love is present in our hearts, then we can overflow with that love to others. It's not our Bible knowledge or amazing evangelistic techniques that make us effective. Bible knowledge is good and techniques can be helpful, but biblically speaking they are no substitute for Christ's love. The Apostle Paul says it unequivocally:

"If I could speak all the languages of earth and of angels, but didn't love others, I would only be a noisy gong or a clanging cymbal. If I had the gift of prophecy, and if I understood all of God's secret plans and possessed all knowledge, and if I had such faith that I could move mountains, but didn't love others, I would be nothing. If I gave everything I have to the poor and even sacrificed my body, I could boast about it; but if I didn't love others, I would have gained nothing" (1 CORINTHIANS 13:1-3).

Maybe you—and many of your family and friends—have had negative experiences with religious people. People who have had lots of ideas and spewed doctrine like there's no tomorrow, but as far as you can tell, they didn't have love. It's hard enough to believe the audacious claims that these people have found "the way, the truth, and the life" (JOHN 14:6) but without tangible seeds of action—seeds that contain the love of Jesus—it's nearly impossible.

For more than 20 years we've been seeking ways to share Jesus with our family and friends—ways that are genuinely refreshing and that flow naturally into the course of daily life. You'll find many of these practical ideas in our other books, especially *Irresistible Evangelism* (Group Publishing, Inc, 2004), but the real secret is *in the seed.* Where there is little seed, there is little harvest. As you share the Good News of Jesus' life, if the seed of Christ's love isn't clearly evident—so people can recognize it for what it is—don't be surprised when your family and friends don't respond positively.

Planted With Love

We've conducted a good bit of research to determine what turns people on and what turns them off, spiritually speaking. One way we conducted this research was to send camera crews out on the streets of major cities to interview ordinary people. We asked people all sorts of questions trying to discern what they thought of Christians who "evangelize." Unfortunately, the most frequent comments we heard contained words like *pushy, rude, arrogant,* and *disrespectful.*

Many people related negative experiences they've had with folks who didn't seem to care enough to listen, and who seemed intent on disrespectfully shoving their beliefs down other people's throats. Instead of sensing God's love in those who were sharing with them, what people reported hearing about most was God's anger. They heard that God was mad at them and—unless they straightened up—they were going to fry!

One young man we filmed echoed this general theme when he sarcastically complained, "They gave me a pamphlet. I read it, threw it in the garbage, and now I'm going to hell! Isn't that just great?" Though the motives of the pamphleteers were no doubt noble, is it such a surprise that Christ's message wasn't getting through to this guy? It may have worked for Jonah back in Old Testament days, but preaching God's wrath against sinners in today's streets is much more likely to get you ignored as an annoying kook than to produce sincere repentance. We wonder why it's so easy to miss the New Testament passage in Romans 2:4 that says God's kindness leads to repentance?

Kindness flows more naturally, but if there is a word on the street about evangelism as it's commonly practiced that word is: *Yuck!* And most of the Christians we've interviewed know it all too well. Though they'll often admit to feeling guilty for not sharing the gospel with their family and friends, in the very next breath those Christians will acknowledge that they'd much rather feel guilty for not evangelizing than alienating the people they care about. Though preachers may attempt to shame and pressure Christians into doing it, they cringe at the very sound of the word *evangelize.* Isn't it weird that sharing the "good news" of Jesus has become "bad news" to both the intended recipients *and* to the messengers appointed to deliver it?

Pollster George Barna points out that though most Christians really want to show Christ's love and bring hope to the lives around them, this is not always—or even usually—what others see. He says, "Regardless of its true character and intent, the Christian community is not known for love nor for a life-transforming faith…" Think about it. How evident are the seeds of Christ's love in your life? How often do your family and friends see—and experience—Christ's love in you?

Seeds of love can often be little acts of kindness we don't think much about at the time. Dave tells a story about the son of one of his fellow teachers back when he was teaching high school.

> As I mentioned earlier in the book, back when I was a high school teacher, my spiritual life wasn't all that I wanted it to be. Fortunately God doesn't need spiritual giants to plant seeds. I know this because of a phone call I got from Brad, the son of a fellow teacher I worked with during those days. I was shocked when he thanked me for introducing him and his best friend, Jeff, to Christ.
>
> "No way!" I said, "I'm thrilled to hear it, but I'm pretty sure I didn't have anything to do with it." Then Brad explained that they both knew I was a Christian because I'd talked about Jesus with them from time to time. But it was lots of little things I'd done—like giving them rides back and forth to school in my Triumph convertible, and lending them albums of the weird Scottish music I liked—that had made them hungry to find out more about a relationship with God. Somehow these seeds I didn't even know I was planting took root. Now Brad has a beautiful Christian wife and family and his good friend Jeff has gone on to become a pastor.

God loves planting seeds in you and through you. If you have Jesus in your life, you have a huge silo of seed ready for distribution. In Chapter 9 we talked about the humble Christians of Elderet, Kenya, who took a Saturday to clean up garbage from the streets. To the extent that they did it with Christ's love, they were flinging little seeds of God's love all over town. Of course one of the best places to begin flinging seeds is your own front lawn—that is, your closest relationships.

Be Indiscriminate

You'll be excited to hear that you don't have to be a salesman or even an extrovert to share Christ's love—you just have to be a really good sower. Perhaps that's why after Jesus told the crowd the basics of sowing, he gave a detailed explanation of exactly what it meant. We're pretty sure it's because he wanted us to know what to expect when we go out there and sow. Here's what he said:

"The seed that fell on the footpath represents those who hear the message about the Kingdom and don't understand it. Then the evil one comes and snatches away the seed that was planted in their hearts. The seed on the rocky soil represents those who hear the message and immediately receive it with joy. But since they don't have deep roots, they don't last long. They fall away as soon as they have problems or are persecuted for believing God's Word. The seed that fell among the thorns represents those who hear God's Word, but all too quickly the message is crowded out by the worries of this life and the lure of wealth, so no fruit is produced. The seed that fell on good soil represents those who truly hear and understand God's Word and produce a harvest of thirty, sixty, or even a hundred times as much as had been planted!" (MATTHEW 13:19-23).

Notice that Jesus doesn't tell you *not* to waste your seed on people whose hearts are concrete-hard pathways of misunderstanding. As we've been saying throughout this book, God's supply is so abundant that it's inexhaustible. Unfortunately, we keep on acting as if the seed of God's love is in precariously short supply. As a result, we sow carefully and sparingly. This totally goes against the Bible's clear teaching that, "Whoever sows sparingly will also reap sparingly, and whoever sows generously will also reap generously" (2 CORINTHIANS 9:6, NIV).

There is no heavenly accountant toting up the number of conversions per dollar's-worth of seed. On the contrary, since there is an endless seed supply, Jesus clearly assumes you're going to fling out lots and lots of Christ's love into hearts that won't grasp it before the Thief comes along and snatches it away. You're called to be such a prodigious, indiscriminate seed flinger that your love goes everywhere. Of course, not every seed will produce a conversion.

Some of your seeds of love will go unnoticed—snatched away by the Thief before anyone even notices them. And some of your loving actions will fall on hearts that are full of spiritual rocks—rocks that make it hard for faith to take lasting root. Perhaps that person was betrayed by a church or has been wounded by a hypocritical Christian relative and his or her heart has been hardened. Another person might be so caught up in the "thorns" of materialism and the anxieties of life that your seeds of love get choked before they can mature. But there will be other times you'll fling seeds of Christ's love on soil that God—and his many *other* servants besides you—have been preparing for just such a moment. And the seeds will take root and grow...and produce fruit.

Looking in from the outside, you can't really tell what kind of soil is in somebody's heart. From the outside, both the authors of this book looked like they were totally closed and even hostile to the gospel. Fortunately, that didn't stop their family and friends from continually planting seeds of God's love and acceptance in their lives.

The next four readings will help you learn some of the ins and outs of sowing Jesus' love into the hearts of those closest to you. Through small acts of kindness, listening, and sharing you can bring your family and friends closer and closer to a relationship with Jesus. We'll talk about practical ways to rebuild burnt relational bridges and to reopen doors that family members and friends have slammed shut. We'll also explain how to invite them to have their own, personal relationship with Jesus—when they're ready.

getting your **feet wet**

What specific seeds of love and kindness have helped to bring you closer to God?

....

....

....

....

How might you sow similar seeds into the lives of your family and friends? Or, to put it another way, what are some natural ways you can let Christ's love overflow into the everyday activities you do with your family and friends? Be as creative and specific as possible.

the **reflection** *pool*

>> What fears or hesitations come to mind when you imagine telling your family and friends about Jesus?

>> What have your experiences of sharing Jesus' love with your family and friends been like?

>> How might "flinging seeds of Jesus' love" change the way your unbelieving family members and friends think of Jesus?

"...TAKE NOTE OF THIS:
EVERYONE SHOULD BE QUICK
TO LISTEN, SLOW TO SPEAK,
AND SLOW TO BECOME
ANGRY."

—JAMES 1:19 (NIV)

"Many people are looking for
an ear that will listen. They
do not find it among Christians,
because these Christians
are talking where they
should be listening."

—Dietrich Bonhoeffer

READING 12

the value of listening

It's a gift that can radically transform you and everyone around you. Though it isn't expensive in terms of money, millions avoid it because they consider it to be too costly. In a world where talk is cheap, *good listening* is still pure gold. And when it comes to showing the love of Jesus to those closest to you, using your ears effectively is always more powerful than running your mouth. We all know this, but knowing it doesn't necessarily translate into doing. Why not?

Many people in modern societies have become extremely impatient with the time and focus required to come to a full understanding of what the people around them are thinking and feeling. They're no-nonsense consumers who want quick answers to all their questions, quick solutions to all their problems, and if they're Christians, they're often looking for quick conversions in the lives of their family members and friends. The author of the book of James was a no-nonsense guy, too. He had the unenviable task of leading the first century church through some of its most powerful and turbulent seasons of growth. James talked about being quick, too, but not in ways most of us like to hear. A man of few words, James spoke with the quiet authority of someone who knew Jesus like a brother, saying, "…take note of this: Everyone should be quick to listen, slow to speak, and slow to become angry" (JAMES 1:19, NIV).

There is a lot of wisdom packed into that one little sentence, so let's break it down. James starts with: *Take note.* These days we'd say something like: *Drop what you are doing and pay attention!* Get rid of all the thousand-and-one things that so easily distract you and focus! Now that James has our undivided attention, he gets right to the point: *Be quick to listen.* In other words, let the first lightning-fast impulse that passes through your brain be to zero in on precisely what the person in front of you is trying to communicate. This quick-to-listen attitude is practically irresistible, and it's one of the most important aspects of letting God's love overflow from you into that next tier of the fountain—your family and friends.

66

Our friend Lisa is a great example of the approach we're talking about here. One Sunday morning a few years back, the outreach pastor from her church approached her to ask if she'd be willing to join his new evangelism team. After considering for a moment, the first words out of her mouth were, "I'm sorry, I'm no good at evangelism!"

Since that's what practically everyone he'd asked had said, he pressed his case a little harder. "Wouldn't it be exciting to help people come to know Jesus?" he asked.

"Oh," Lisa replied with a big smile, "I get to do that all the time!"

When the pastor asked what she meant, Lisa explained:

"Every few months God sends me a new friend to listen to. Pretty much all I do is tune in to what's going on in that person's life and let the person know that I care. Sooner or later, for some reason I don't really understand, most of those people ask me how to get to know Jesus. When they do, I tell them. And then we pray together to ask the Lord to come into their hearts. I can't stand the idea of doing that high-pressure knocking on doors evangelism thing; it feels too manipulative to me. But I love connecting with people heart to heart."

After a moment of stunned silence, the pastor rocked back his head and roared with laughter. He'd been swimming upstream trying to get people in his church past their fear of sharing Jesus—but obviously Lisa could teach him a thing or two. Once he collected himself, he asked, "Just out of curiosity, how many people are we talking about?"

All Lisa could say in the moment was that she'd led so many people to the Lord she'd lost count. But when she went home that evening her pastor's question spurred her to look through her personal journals from the previous seven years. When she was done, she realized that she'd befriended, listened to, and helped more than 80 people begin a personal relationship with Jesus! Though she still doesn't think she's any good at evangelism, Lisa is so quick to listen that God keeps on sending her more and more friends. And as they get to know Lisa, naturally they get to know Jesus, too.

Noticing

If you want to be as quick to listen as Lisa, it's best to get started before the person in front of you ever opens his or her mouth. We call this *the ministry of noticing*. Just pay close attention to the person you're with, and you'll begin to notice subtle body language that clues you in to what that person is feeling. You'll notice whether the person looks happy or sad or worried or confused— and as he or she begins to talk, you'll already be well on your way to entering your friend's world. As words begin flowing, put your own reactions aside so you can pay very close attention to what the person is saying. Without moving your lips, try mentally translating what he or she is saying into your own words. If there is a pause in the conversation every now and then, check in verbally to make sure you understand what your friend is saying.

Lisa said she didn't understand why the people around her ended up talking about spiritual things so often when all she did was listen. If we were to hazard a guess, it's probably because the listening she does is a *spiritual* act. No matter what subject a friend or family member is talking about, laying down your agenda is a small way of dying to yourself and acting more like Jesus. This is easy to say, but how do you practice dying to self? A good first step is to tell yourself that what's happening is *not about you*. What it's about is showing the person you're listening to God's love in one of the most practical ways possible: truly listening. By laying down your own needs and interests for a little while, you are in essence saying, "I'm here for you and care deeply about what's important to you." And by extension, "God cares, too."

It takes discipline to focus, but it's not just an act or a psychological technique. It's being fully receptive to the person talking and treating that person with the kind of compassion and respect that says, "As far as I'm concerned, you're the most interesting and important person in this room." For most people this kind of listening is not only irresistible, it's indistinguishable from deep friendship and love.

If your friend is talking about a new job opportunity and seems pretty excited about it, and you chime in with something like, "Wow, you sound really pumped about this!" you are rejoicing with those who rejoice (ROMANS 12:15a). Usually that person will respond enthusiastically and continue talking with you about the new job. Other times that person might open a window into fears or insecurities he or she hasn't mentioned to anyone else. Perhaps taking this new job will mean moving or leaving important friendships behind. In this case, your listening might become mourning with those who mourn (ROMANS 12:15b) as you express your sympathy or offer to pray for the person.

Once people see that you genuinely care, they tend to open up the door to more vulnerable stuff that's on their mind.

Acceptance Is Not Endorsement

When this happens, it's difficult for many—especially extroverts—to put challenging questions and editorial comments on hold. That's why James's next point is to *be slow to speak*. Unfortunately many of us (especially those who've grown up in religious families or gone to legalistic churches) feel an overwhelming need to parent or scold anyone who says something that doesn't line up with what we've been taught. Instead of listening, we take every opportunity to disagree or correct any beliefs and behaviors we find unacceptable. Given this predisposition to *pre-emptively disagree* with what they think, their lifestyle choices, and even the kind of music they enjoy; it's no wonder so many not-yet Christians see us as *disagreeable people.*

Being slow to speak is not only much kinder and more respectful, it goes a long way toward overcoming this perception of disagreeability. Many Christians feel uncomfortable allowing other people to air what they truly feel and believe because Christians don't want those people to get the impression they're endorsing sin. As our friend Randy Bolender often says, "We confuse acceptance with endorsement. Just because we accept somebody doesn't mean we endorse everything they've ever said…Acceptance is not endorsement."

Miriam, who'd grown up in a very conservative religious household, discovered the power of this idea a few years ago.

> When Miriam's younger sister, Sarah, got divorced, rejected the faith she'd been raised in, and moved in with an atheist boyfriend; the rest of her family cut Sarah off. Some thought even talking to Sarah while she was choosing to live in sin amounted to endorsing her wayward behavior. Her mother said she was willing to talk to Sarah on the phone but made it clear that Sarah and her boyfriend were not welcome at family gatherings.
>
> Miriam did not approve of her younger sister's choices either, but she wanted to continue being part of Sarah's life and to keep reaching out to her. So instead of shunning Sarah and avoiding the boyfriend, Miriam visited them both more than ever before. Miriam made a point of listening to her sister as Sarah poured out her heart and shared the feelings of rejection she was experiencing from her ex-husband and most of her family. Miriam chose to be slow to speak about what she viewed as her sister's spiritually unhealthy choices. Even though Miriam was tempted from time to time, she refrained from giving moral lectures. The fact was Sarah already knew Miriam didn't endorse all her actions; but more importantly, Sarah knew—and experienced—Miriam's unconditional love for her.
>
> By the time a year had passed, Sarah and her boyfriend had changed dramatically. Both were actively checking out Miriam's church and taking a premarital seminar. Today, not only are they married, but—in no

small part due to Miriam's steadfast listening—both they and their children are happily following Jesus. Miriam's love for Jesus had overflowed into Sarah's life—changing Sarah's heart along with the hearts of her whole family. It wasn't easy by a long shot, but Miriam's compassionate listening without endorsement healed her family.

Being slow to put your two cents in is not only biblical; it allows the person who is talking to keep control of the direction and pace of the conversation. We can't overstate the importance of being slow to speak in spiritual conversations—or those that might someday move in a spiritual direction. Good listening is like pouring water on the thirsty seeds of love we talked about in the last reading. Seeds just naturally respond to it.

The Love Test

As anyone who has living relatives knows, not everyone is easy to listen to. That's why once you've schooled yourself in listening quickly and talking slowly, it's time to look at James' final admonition: *Be slow to become angry.* This one is especially hard when you're listening to someone who knows exactly where all your hot buttons are…and precisely how to push them. And push them that person usually will—right when you're in the middle of trying to show compassion and patience.

That person might do it by mocking or putting down the things you hold most dear, or bringing up some sore spot between the two of you. We call this kind of behavior a "love test." Though that person probably isn't conscious about doing it, he or she seems to delight in tweaking you in emotionally vulnerable places and watching you squirm. And though it's no fun for you as a listener, it quite often comes right before that person invites you into places he or she normally guards or hides from others.

The secret to passing a love test is usually to be quick to listen to God's heart for that person, and slow to internalize the provocative words. In other words: Love that person like God does—and don't take his or her words personally! It'll take great self-control not to grab the bait being dangled in front of your nose, but passing it up can lead to some pretty exciting places. In the story we told earlier, Miriam's sister would constantly try to goad her into an angry outburst. Sarah would talk about the benefits of living with her boyfriend before marriage, or speak enthusiastically of her new atheistic beliefs. But what Miriam knew—and what we all have to recognize as we're in these situations—is that this was Sarah's love test. Sarah had been rejected and abandoned by all the other Christians in her life and she expected the same thing from Miriam. She wanted to throw the worst at Miriam to test her love and see if Miriam would still stick around. Though it was difficult—and though she had to deny herself over and over again—Miriam passed her sister's love tests.

But if your family and close friends are anything like ours, you probably won't always succeed. You'll sometimes have to back up and apologize by saying something like, "I'm sorry, this is a tender spot for me, but I really want to understand where you're coming from." It's humbling, but the relational tension you'll experience is a little bit like what happens to an airplane as it approaches the speed of sound. The closer that airplane gets to the sound-barrier, the more it feels like vibrations and turbulence are going to tear the plane apart. But once the plane passes through that barrier, the flight is much faster and smoother. Once you get past the love test, the listening will get easier and the relationship better.

Becoming Salt and Light

Jesus could possibly have been talking about the idea of a love test when he said, "God blesses you when people mock you and persecute you and lie about you and say all sorts of evil things against you because you are my followers" (MATTHEW 5:11). Reaching out with the love of Jesus often contains within it the risk of being offended and mistreated by the very people for whom you are sacrificing. The reality is if you act like Jesus, sometimes people will treat you like they treated him. It doesn't always feel good in the moment, but in the long run it's full of blessing. It's one little part of being the salt of the earth and the light of the world (MATTHEW 5:13-15)—something we'll talk more about in the next reading.

getting your feet wet

Listen to a friend or family member for five minutes without reacting, directing, or correcting them. See if they respond any differently than usual. If they do, keep it up and see if it changes the spiritual climate of your relationship.

the reflection pool

>>When have you felt like someone was *really* listening to you? What was that like?

>>How has true listening changed a relationship for the better in your life? Or how might it in the future?

>>Who do you find it hardest to really listen to? How can you practice sincerely listening to that person in the way this chapter describes?

"LET YOUR LIGHT SHINE
BEFORE MEN, THAT THEY MAY
SEE YOUR GOOD
DEEDS AND PRAISE YOUR
FATHER IN HEAVEN."

—MATTHEW 5:16 (NIV)

"It is no use walking
anywhere to preach unless our
walking is our preaching."

—St. Francis of Assisi

READING 13

loving family and friends toward Jesus

A couple of very zealous Christian students noticed a frazzled-looking husband and wife sitting in a car with a flat tire. As the students walked up to the car, the more extroverted of them said something that went like this:

"Hi. We see you have a flat tire." After pausing for dramatic effect, the student went on, "Did you ever stop to think what would have happened if you'd slammed into that telephone pole over there and been killed when your tire blew?" After pausing once again to let that grisly image sink in, he inquired, "If you'd died, do you think you would have gone to heaven or hell?"

The unhappy driver and his wife were both nearly speechless with the shock of their accident, and what they perceived as an unprovoked "evangelistic" assault. But eventually the husband reined in his temper long enough to mumble something like, "Thanks for your concern. Please don't worry about us." After this exchange, the young men abruptly walked away, no doubt thinking they'd given the unfortunate couple some deep spiritual truth to chew on. Perhaps in their minds they'd just had a great "witnessing" experience. Sadly, these students who apparently felt such deep concern for the couple's eternal destination didn't seem to care enough to offer any help in changing the flat tire!

Instead of drawing the couple closer to Christ with their provocative questions, the students' unwitting insensitivity had planted seeds of resentment against Christ and his church that could have persisted for many years. Fortunately there's more to the story. Our friend Steve tells us what happened years later when he met up with the same couple.

"I was sad, and a little disgusted on God's behalf, as my two friends angrily told me the story of the 'flat-tire evangelists.' At that point I'd been quietly trying to get to know this couple, and for several months we'd been talking together about spiritual questions they had. As they relayed the flat-tire story, the new question on their minds went something like this: 'How can some Christians be so obnoxious? And why are you so different...so much friendlier?' "

The good news is that instead of simply being victims of a "drive-by evangelism attack," the couple had a contrasting experience with Steve—one in which they were truly able to see the overflowing love of Jesus. Steve had been persistently reaching out and modeling openness, honesty, and respect to them. He'd listened to their questions and criticisms of Christianity without becoming defensive or pushy. And though Steve was very open about his faith, he was a fun person and real friend. In fact, not very long after the conversation above, the couple started attending a course for religious skeptics offered at Steve's church. They still have many questions but they've realized that they want Jesus in their lives.

We wonder what might have happened if the college students had rolled up their sleeves and offered to change the couple's tire before attempting to question their eternal life. The students might have had a better chance to make a positive connection—one in which real dialogue could have naturally unfolded without anyone feeling attacked or condemned.

James put it this way, "What good is it, dear brothers and sisters, if you say you have faith but don't show it by your actions? Can that kind of faith save anyone? Suppose you see a brother or sister who has no food or clothing, and you say, "Good-bye and have a good day; stay warm and eat well"—but then you don't give that person any food or clothing. What good does that do?" (JAMES 2:14-16).

If your goal is to share the love of Jesus with those closest to you, doesn't it make sense to lead off with friendly actions and follow up with loving words? Like Steve, you can help those around you—even those who've had unpleasant experiences—see Christ and his church in a different light!

Light and Salt

Jesus said, "While I am here in the world, *I* am the light of the world" (JOHN 9:5, emphasis added). And on another occasion he explained, "*You* are the light of the world" (MATTHEW 5:14, emphasis added).

So which is it? Is Jesus the light or are we? The simple, straightforward, only somewhat confusing answer is, "We both are!" One of the reasons Jesus came to earth was to shed light on the true personality and character of God. When the Apostle Philip asked him, "Lord, show us the Father, and we will be satisfied" (JOHN 14:8). Jesus replied: "Have I been with you all this time, Philip, and yet you still don't know who I am? Anyone who has seen me has seen the Father!" (JOHN 14:9).

Jesus lived to reveal the contents of God's heart to us, as a lamp exists to reveal the contents of a darkened room. Without Jesus, we can't really "see" God *or* our true selves. You can't live as God intends without his light any more than you can walk a perfectly straight line in complete darkness. Without light, you would perpetually stub your toes on hidden obstacles, fall down and hurt yourself, or worst of all, wound others. But in the time it takes to flip on a switch—or offer a prayer—Jesus' light can dispel darkness and show you the path ahead.

Our lives have no inborn light source of their own, but when we follow

Jesus closely, we reflect some of his light. Maybe you've run into a few people in your life who seem to shine with hope and compassion. They light up any room with friendliness and joy reflected from their inner connection with God. Steve, our friend in the story earlier, is one of those people. The couple he was reaching out to saw and felt God's kindness reflected through him. This is what Jesus was talking about when he said, "A city on a hill cannot be hidden. Neither do people light a lamp and put it under a bowl. Instead they put it on its stand, and it gives light to everyone in the house. In the same way, let your light shine before men, that they may see your good deeds and praise your Father in heaven" (MATTHEW 5:14b-16, NIV).

Apparently, unlike the moon, which reflects the sun's rays whether it wants to or not, it's possible for us to hide or eclipse the light we've been given. But why would we ever do such a thing?

Well, for one, light in the darkness draws attention like orange blossoms draw bees. If you shine with the light of Jesus, like it or not, you'll be noticed. You'll bring attention and praise to the Father in heaven, and—even if you don't mean to—you'll draw attention to yourself as well. This wouldn't be so scary if you could perfectly reflect the Savior's light all of the time, but—frail human creatures that we all are—you probably have a few flaws and weaknesses you'd rather hide in the shadows than allow others to see.

As wonderful as the light is, it does have a habit of revealing blemishes and flaws in such a way that makes them hard to ignore. Just as the sun reveals the craters and fissures on the moon for all to see, so Jesus' light will have the tendency of revealing your weaknesses and imperfections. The more light that's in your life, the more you'll find yourself having to acknowledge your transgressions and, like King David, confess, "For I recognize my rebellion; it haunts me day and night" (PSALM 51:3). Though God certainly loves you—pimples, warts, muddy face, and all—that doesn't mean you always like what you see in his perfect mirror. In some ways, hiding your light under a bushel is akin to a 2-year-old with a dirty face closing her eyes and pretending she's invisible instead of allowing her parents to wash her face. As a grown-up, you probably know that if you hide your problems from yourself and others, they're more likely to get worse than to go away on their own.

There is something incredibly attractive and fresh about people who readily admit and fearlessly address their besetting faults—people who, with

God's help, work to overcome those faults. Though it's not something religious people are typically known for, being open about your struggles and vulnerable with your weaknesses, gives others permission to admit they need help in some of the very same areas. As you continually come to God for help and begin living in ways that overflow with his goodness, others will notice there's something different going on in your life. Like it or not, friends and family members will probably be the first to notice.

They'll be watching and perhaps even testing your resolve to become more like Jesus. Barbara told us this story about Robin, the family babysitter her little son and her whole family nicknamed "Bin Bin."

Barbara had been raised in a tightknit Jewish community where she picked up the idea that non-Jews, and especially Christians were *never* to be trusted. Barbara describes how the light Bin Bin brought with her, changed how Barbara thought about Jesus:

> Bin Bin is everything I'm not. She is quiet, self-effacing, and intensely shy. Normally I wouldn't have paid much attention to her, but during my son's first year, she became very important in my life. On many occasions she would drive all the way across town to drop off a prescription for me or just to provide a few quiet words of comfort. After months of benefiting from her quiet kindness, I finally asked her why she was so different. She told me it was Jesus, and for the first time in my life, I really listened.

> Bin Bin was different from anyone I'd ever met—Christian or Jew. I wanted to discover what made her so special, so I started attending her church. I knew the events of my life were converging to a single moment. I finally surrendered my heart to Bin Bin's Jesus. Now I just want to reach out quietly, gently, and unobtrusively for God's glory, just like Bin Bin!

There was no hard sell, no provocative turn-or-burn confrontation here. Robin just let her light shine. And even though she was shy, when the opportunity came to explain why she was so different, she bravely stood up and gave all the credit to Jesus. Robin's story demonstrates what Peter was talking about when he said, "But in your hearts set apart Christ as Lord. Always be prepared to give an answer to everyone who asks you to give the reason for the hope that you have. But do this with gentleness and respect" (1 PETER 3:15-16a, NIV). It's amazing how many well-meaning people miss both the "everyone who asks" and the "gentleness and respect" parts of this verse.

We're not saying words aren't necessary, just that usually they need a context in which to be understood and received. If you love friends and family members in practical ways first, while living your faith openly and honestly in front of them, they *will* start to have questions. If they see you working to forgive those who wrong you, loving people others ignore, and following Jesus in other ways that "aren't normal," they'll become curious. They'll wonder what's wrong with you...or what's right with you. Either way, people who are asking questions are much more open to answers than people who are simply having answers forced on them, whether they care or not.

Overflowing with God's love and joy will invite questions and open opportunities for you to share your hope with those you love.

Of course, one really big reason many of us are tempted to hide our lights is because we're afraid of others judging us. Though most are drawn to it, not everyone enjoys the light of Christ. Sometimes even the kindest and most loving behavior can irritate people or rub them the wrong way. Maybe this is why Jesus gives us yet another picture to describe Christians: "You are the salt of the earth," he said in Matthew 5:13. Like light, salt is something every human being needs to be healthy. It adds zest to our lives and savor to our food. And anyone who has ever gargled salt water for a sore throat knows that it has healing properties. But anyone who has gotten salt in an open wound also knows how much it can sting. If you love Jesus, and don't hide it, the fact is you will draw praise from some and harsh criticism from others—some people you will sting.

A number of those whose lives bear open emotional wounds—especially those who've had negative experiences related to religion—can react harshly to salt. They may mock you or attack you even as you seek to unselfishly serve them. There is a spiritual battle going on inside their souls, and you can easily get caught in the crossfire. You're likely to catch flack that has more to do with their past experiences and prejudices than anything you've personally done. If you're not being preachy and judgmental, then it's not your fault if your salty behavior stings them and triggers anger and defensiveness. Though it's no fun to be on the receiving end of negative reactions, we want to encourage you: *please, do not stop.*

Before Dave asked Jesus to come into his heart, he was often nasty toward the Christians who tried to befriend him.

> Even though the Thief was working overtime to try and keep me miserable, my longing to receive their kindness grew in spite of the chilly reception I continually gave them. It's strange how angry resistance and confused longing can live so close together inside the same person, but that's how it was with me.
>
> Those "dorky Christians" showed me such great love, joy, peace, patience, kindness, goodness, faithfulness, gentleness, and self-control that I got thirstier and thirstier every day. Though I tried to reject them and drive them away, it was only a matter of time before I began asking questions and seeking God for myself.
>
> I hate to think what might have happened if they'd given up.

Being light and salt isn't just something you do—it becomes a fundamental part of *who you are*. You *are* the light and you *are* the salt as you let Jesus work in you and as you let others see what he's doing in you. As you tap into his fountain and allow his life to pour through you and overflow into the lives of your family and friends—you'll become different. And because you're different, you'll act differently, too. A big part of that change is developing an empathetic and understanding heart—something we'll talk more about in the next reading.

getting your **feet wet**

Think of a family member or a friend you would like to reach with a small touch of God's love.

Tell God who you are thinking about and ask him to help you come up with some small action that could communicate his love to that person. It could be an invitation to lunch, an offer to go fishing, or just a phone call to say, "I was praying for you and wondered how things are going in your life."

Whatever idea comes to mind, don't put it off; go ahead and give it a try and see what happens.

the **reflection** *pool*

>> Think of a negative and a positive experience you've had with Christians—how did those two interactions affect your perception of Jesus and the church?

>> When is it hard for you to be salt and light to those around you? Why do you think that is?

>> What can you do *tomorrow* to be salt and light to your family and friends?

"I PLANTED THE SEED IN YOUR HEARTS, AND APOLLOS WATERED IT, BUT IT WAS GOD WHO MADE IT GROW. IT'S NOT IMPORTANT WHO DOES THE PLANTING, OR WHO DOES THE WATERING. WHAT'S IMPORTANT IS THAT GOD MAKES THE SEED GROW."

—1 CORINTHIANS 3:6-7

"God has made a rule for himself that he won't alter people's character by force. He can and will alter them—but only if the people will let him."

—C.S. Lewis, *God in the Dock*

READING 14

sharing Jesus with those you love

We've traveled the world and communicated with thousands of people from many different cultures. We've been in places where nodding your head up and down means "no" instead of "yes" and where lighting up a big, fat, smelly cigar in church after a service is considered the height of good manners. In our travels we've also noticed how friends and family members who grew up in the same city, attended the same schools, and even shared the same parents, are often so different they seem as if they've been rocketed to earth from entirely different planets. If there's one thing we've learned, it's that—whether we realize it or not—*spiritual communication is cross-cultural.*

Sharing Empathy

As close as you might be to someone in other ways, your spiritual path has been shaped by experiences that are utterly unique to you. It's easy to assume that your worldview and unique way of seeing things is "the right one," and that those closest to you will eventually embrace it because it's so obvious. This is one reason so many people who haven't come to Jesus yet see their Christian friends or relatives as "narrow-minded." When they look at those Christians, they perceive no empathy or willingness to dialogue. And it's a major turnoff.

We often use this hands-on exercise to help people come to grips with the fruitlessness of insisting their way of seeing things is the only way.

All you have to do is stand face-to-face with another person, hold your hands up, and press your palms into that person's palms. Look the person in the eye and say simply, "I'm right!" The other person should respond by forcefully saying, "No, I'm right!" Go back and forth a few times. If you're like most people who've tried this, pretty soon you'll begin pushing the other person away and then that person will begin pushing you back. Meanwhile, with increasing volume, you'll continue shouting at each other about how "right" you are.

Since everyone perceives the world in his or her own unique way, most people have a tendency to believe their way of seeing and thinking is "the right way." It's a general lack of empathy. And sadly, these days bringing God and the Bible into the argument on your side will rarely produce the results you're hoping for—no matter how well-spoken you are or how good you are at debate.

As far as the person on the receiving-end of your argument is concerned, you're just pushing back against what he or she believes with more of what you believe. Most arguments of this sort end in a stalemate with everyone exasperated and irritated. Does this sound anything like what you've experienced in your discussions with friends and family who aren't yet Christians?

It's one thing to be the light of the world and the salt of the earth, making people thirsty for Jesus, but it's quite another to be irritating and argumentative. One of the most important things we can share with our nonbelieving family and friends is empathy.

Please don't get us wrong. We believe that Jesus is "the way, the truth, and the life" and that nobody comes to the Father except through him (JOHN 14:6). However, we've seen many, many more people "loved into" God's kingdom than "argued in." We're not saying it can't happen, just that in our experience there's a much wiser and more effective approach. If we pause the "hands-on" exercise we described earlier for a moment and make a minor adjustment to the approach—adding a bit of empathy—you'll be amazed at the difference it makes. Here's what you can do. Instead of countering the other person's assertion with an even louder assertion of your own, try asking a simple question instead. Say something like "Help me understand what you're saying."

When you do this, the person will probably tell you he or she is right a few more times—each time less and less forcefully. Eventually, if that person really believes you want to understand—and if you confine yourself to listening to and clarifying what that person is saying, rather than arguing—you'll probably be amazed at how quickly the tension dissipates. Once you show real interest in building a bridge to that person's world, and a desire to understand how that person arrived at his or her beliefs, then a conversation can begin. Your new friend may even invite you to explain what you've come to believe. Sharing mutual empathy. Sharing mutual respect. It's the first step to sharing Jesus with your family and friends—and it avoids a lot of potentially disastrous misunderstandings.

A pastor we know describes a huge misstep he made while trying to share the good news of Jesus with the people around him.

Back in the mid-1970s (days of intense racial unrest in Alabama) some friends of mine decided they wanted to "witness for Jesus" out in front of the bars and strip clubs of downtown Pensacola, Florida. Someone from the group suggested that a good way to share with the people along this strip would be to carry a cross as we walked back and forth downtown and prayed. When it was my turn to carry the cross, something happened that's been burned into my memory ever since.

I was walking along Palafox Street carrying that 6-foot cross and leading a few brave prayer warriors behind me. When I came to a crosswalk, a dignified black man stepped in front of me and pulled back his coat to reveal a pearl-handled .38 special. In a quiet but ominous voice he drawled, "KKK boy?"

"No sir," I stammered, utter terror filling my words, "We're just Christians walking around with a cross and...uh...praying for the city—we never thought...uh...I'm sorry if we've offended you in any way, sir!"

Casting me a look of intense disgust, he rolled his eyes, closed his coat to cover the gun, and quietly walked away.

This encounter wasn't just terrifying; it was a defining moment for my life and my ministry. That night I realized communicating the gospel isn't just a matter of how positive my intentions are. *What others perceive and believe matters as much or more!*

The need to demonstrate that you're right can obscure the good news of Jesus' love all together. After all, in the end, it's not about winning arguments, it's about winning people's hearts. Maybe that's why—as we've pointed out before—Romans 2:4 asks, "Don't you realize that God's *kindness* is meant to turn you away from your sins?" (NIRV, emphasis added). It's not a winning debate, or a carefully structured argument that will turn people away from sins—it's God's kindness, flowing through you. Those who are close to us can be some of the hardest people to convince anyway—don't let competitive arguments and never-ending debates make it even harder.

Sharing the Wonder

One of the keys to sharing Jesus' love with people is to share in their wonder of the world. We call it "Active Wondering." It's taking the things you've heard others say and *wondering about them out loud*. Again, we're not talking about arguing or challenging—we're talking about sharing empathy and then going one step further…to open up new possibilities in the conversation. If you've been listening to your brother talk about visiting colleges with his kids, you might share the wonder by saying something like:

"As you've been talking about your kids, I've been wondering what your dreams are for their lives."

Though this may not sound particularly spiritual, you'll be surprised by how quickly spiritual things come into the conversation when you engage people's imaginations. Wondering is spiritual by its very nature. In gardening terms, it stirs up the soil and rouses seeds that have remained dormant for years. It's exciting to see what sprouts pop up as loved ones begin wondering, seeking, and knocking for themselves.

After all, everyone wonders about the big questions of life. They wonder if there is a God and what he might be like. You can join with them in their exploration by asking things like "If God exists, what do you think he's like? What makes God happy or sad? What questions would you like to ask God?" There are hundreds of great opened-ended questions you can ask to spur wonder—questions that will engage your loved one and help you share in the excitement of discovering God together.

Once your friends and family members see you aren't trying to direct the conversation in order to "make a sale," you'll find most of them are very excited to wonder with you. And don't be afraid if questions come up you can't answer. Just simply say, "Wow, I don't know the answer to that one. Let me think about it and get back to you." If this happens, rejoice! You've engaged someone you care about in asking, seeking, and knocking on God's door. And, as you share the wonder with one another, you're discovering more about God's nature…together.

You have a role to play, but God is even more interested than you are in providing answers, helping people find what they're looking for, and opening doors of faith they can step through.

And, keep in mind that no matter what we do, sometimes those closest to us are the most hesitant to respond to what we have to say.

Jesus remarked on this saying, "A prophet is honored everywhere except in his own hometown and among his relatives and his own family" (MARK 6:4). The unfortunate truth is, even if we're as eloquent and profound as the biblical prophets—and even if we share all the empathy and wonder in the world—the people closest to us still might not respond.

Sharing the Process

Here's some great news for everyone struggling to bring a friend or family member to Jesus: *It's not all up to you!* Though you may be tempted to believe that you're the only one who can do the job, God himself is knocking on that person's heart. The Apostle Paul explained this profound truth saying, "I planted the seed in your hearts, and Apollos watered it, but it was God who made it grow" (1 CORINTHIANS 3:6). This verse makes it very clear that God wants us to *share the process* of bringing people into a relationship with

Jesus. You may plant some seeds in your friend or family member's life, other Christians in that person's workplace or neighborhood may then water those seeds, and yet another Christian may end up being the person to harvest the seeds. Your job is clearly to fling lots and lots of seeds whenever you get the opportunity. Your job is to also *water* seeds others have planted. Seeds of kindness need the water of prayer, listening, and friendship. And you may also get the opportunity to harvest some seeds—to see people begin that friendship with Jesus.

But ultimately—no matter who does the watering, planting, or harvesting of those seeds—it's God who makes them grow. Here's a story of what happened in Dave's life.

> One of my closest friends in college was Merry, a young woman who periodically endured what has come to be called bipolar disorder. Her symptoms often included very intense, euphoric episodes when she'd completely lose touch with reality followed by periods when she'd plummet into suicidal depression.
>
> One day Merry showed up at my house and I could see she was in tremendous distress. When I asked Merry what was wrong, she crumpled into a chair and began tearfully confessing to a long list of sins she was sure were "unforgivable." She poured out story after story about what a mess she thought she'd made of her life. After a few hours she was "talked-out" and "cried-out." So I gave her a huge hug and reminded her how much I loved her, and tried to let her know that God's love and forgiveness were greater than any of her sins. I explained that God desperately wanted to help her put the shattered pieces of her life back together.
>
> As Merry walked out my door that night, I felt like a terrible failure. Even though I'd prayed for wisdom and tried with every ounce of love and Bible knowledge I could summon to help her see God's love, nothing had gotten through to her. I'd come to the end of myself, so I fell on my knees and pleaded with God to send her someone who *could* get through to her.
>
> Two days later I was devastated when I received the terrible news that Merry had overdosed on pills and very nearly succeeded in killing herself.

I rushed to see her in the hospital, only to find she was still in a catatonic state. Not knowing what else to do, I read to her from the Bible and from C.S. Lewis' *Chronicles of Narnia* as she stared blankly out into space.

When Louise, one of the nurses on Merry's unit, noticed the Bible and the Narnia books on Merry's nightstand, she began reaching out to Merry with the love of Jesus. Without knowing it, Louise's compassionate actions were watering seeds that I—and many others—had been planting in Merry's heart. Like me, Louise listened carefully and then told Merry God loved her and wanted to forgive all her sins. And just like me, Louise explained God's promise of abundant, overflowing life. Only this time Merry responded!

When Merry was ready to leave the hospital she moved into a house with some of Louise's Christian friends. I'll never forget the phone call I got from Merry announcing that she was getting baptized! It seemed far too good to be true, and I'll admit I was skeptical at the time, but God had answered my prayers. In the hospital Merry got treatment and medication to take care of her illness, but she also found the healer of her soul.

I planted the seeds, and Louise watered them, but it was God who made them grow.

If you don't take anything else from this chapter, remember this: *God loves the people you love even more than you do—and God is even more invested in reaching them than you are.* Only God is not limited by our limitations. God puts us in families and brings people into our lives who we can gently nudge toward God—no matter where they are on their spiritual journey. Some will be close to finding God and others will be farther away. But just as it's a mistake to assume you have no role in helping others toward God, it's also a big mistake to think it's all up to you.

Sharing the Water

The more God pours his living water into you and the more you let that love overflow into the lives of those around you, the more excited and less inhibited you'll be in sharing. The thirsty people around you will naturally begin watching you to try and figure out where your supply of living water is coming from. Though they may not believe what you're saying at first, keep on loving, listening, and wondering with them. Watch for opportunities to overflow into their lives and let God guide and direct you in how best to serve them wherever they are in their journey to God. That's what we'll talk about in the next reading: How you can serve those who are close to you—and in doing so, help them become closer to Jesus.

getting your **feet wet**

Make a list of open-ended, non-threatening questions about God that you can ask your family and friends.

Pray over your list and ask God to help you be empathetic and understanding of where people are coming from when you talk to them. Ask God to open your eyes to times when you can wonder with people—asking them questions from your list or other questions about God that fit naturally in your conversations.

Finally, finish your prayer by asking God to fill the lives of friends and family members with other Christians who are actively planting and watering seeds of God's love.

the **reflection** *pool*

>> Where do you think your friends and family members are in their openness to the gospel? Describe where you think they might be, spiritually speaking, at the moment.

>> What is one way you could share empathy, kindness, and wonder with them in ways that would draw them closer to God?

>> Who else in your friends' and family members' lives are sharing Jesus with them also? How can you support and encourage those Christians as they share the process with you?

READING 15

serving wholeheartedly

When you set out to serve your family and friends in ways that draw them closer to Christ, if there's one thing you can count on, it's that it won't be convenient. Our English word *service* bears this out. It derives from *servus*, the Latin word for *slave*. If by slavery we mean working incredibly hard for someone else's benefit without receiving pay or appreciation, then loving others is positively a completely voluntary form of slavery. When we serve, we choose to surrender our freedom to do whatever we feel like doing in order to do what's best for someone else. As we said, it's seldom convenient. But it can have miraculous results.

The Transforming Power of Service

The first miracle of Jesus as recorded in the Gospel of John was an unselfish act of service to his mother. Mary, Jesus, and his disciples were guests at a wedding in the village of Cana in Galilee. John doesn't identify who the bride or the groom are, only what Mary asked of Jesus when the host family ran out of wine.

> When the wine was gone, Jesus' mother said to him, "They have no more wine."
>
> "Dear woman, why do you involve me?" Jesus replied. "My time has not yet come."
>
> His mother said to the servants, "Do whatever he tells you."
>
> Nearby stood six stone water jars, the kind used by the Jews for ceremonial washing, each holding from twenty to thirty gallons.
>
> Jesus said to the servants, "Fill the jars with water"; so they filled them to the brim.
>
> Then he told them, "Now draw some out and take it to the master of the banquet."
>
> They did so, and the master of the banquet tasted the water that had been turned into wine. He did not realize where it had come from, though the servants who had drawn the water knew. Then he called the bridegroom aside and said, "Everyone brings out the choice wine first and then the cheaper wine after the guests have had too much to drink; but you have saved the best till now."
>
> This, the first of his miraculous signs, Jesus performed in Cana of Galilee. He thus revealed his glory, and his disciples put their faith in him (JOHN 2:4-11, NIV).

If you could turn water into wine, wouldn't you want to grab this golden opportunity to show off your power? Apparently Jesus didn't think so. It's clear he didn't believe it was the right time to reveal what he could do. Though it doesn't appear in the text, we can only imagine the subtle communication that went back and forth between Mary and Jesus after he voiced his objection. Theirs must have been the sort of relationship where words weren't needed in order to discern each other's hearts. Perhaps the gentle smile spreading across Jesus' face told Mary that he was willing to change his plans. If there had been words, maybe Jesus would have said something like, "OK, I'll readjust my divine timetable—that I've had in place for eons—*just to show my love for you.*"

Mary's request wasn't convenient, but it came from a heart filled with kindness. How could he *not* honor her loving impulse? Turning water into wine—it's what serving is all about. It's taking some humble, day-to-day action like washing the dishes in the sink or listening to someone's problems and transforming it into an act of love. In the same way Jesus turned plain old water into a remarkably good vintage of wine, he wants us to transform tiny thoughtful actions into messages that say, "God loves you and so do I!"

Humble Acts of Service

Serving your family and friends doesn't usually consist of grand gestures like buying lavish gifts or taking them on an all-expense-paid vacation. No. It's usually the little stuff that makes the biggest difference. As Mother Teresa put it, "It's not the magnitude of our actions but the amount of love we put into them that matters." God transforms each humble act of service we offer in his name into a miraculous opportunity for the one who receives it. As Scottish theologian William Barclay once explained, "More people are brought into the church by the kindness of real Christian love than by all the theological arguments in the world." In fact, humbly serving those closest to us is probably the most persuasive theological "argument" of all.

As we conduct workshops on evangelism all over the globe, we often ask folks to raise their hands to indicate how they came to faith in Jesus. In most groups, less than five of every 100 people indicate they came to Christ through a combination of evangelistic revivals, crusades, television or radio preaching, Christian books, or Bible tracts. On average, more than 95 percent indicate that a personal relationship with a Christian close to them is what brought them to Jesus. Think about what that means for a minute: Your personal relationships are potentially more powerful than Billy Graham, the very best TV and radio preachers you've ever heard, and the most profound Christian authors you've ever read—all rolled into one!

We've always believed that just about any evangelism is good evangelism, so we aren't putting down any of the ministries or methods mentioned above. That's not our point. Our point is that *you* have an amazingly powerful influence—if you're willing to use it.

It's not always convenient, but it can be incredibly fun and fulfilling. Don't worry, we aren't asking you to be pushy or obnoxious. On the contrary, we're hoping you'll become an active goodwill ambassador for Jesus in your own home, at your workplace, and with your friends. *Active* is a critical term because there is little or no fruit in being a passive, silent Christian. When Jesus turned water into wine there were immediate, tangible results. The Bible says when Jesus "revealed his glory...his disciples put their faith in him" (JOHN 2:11b, NIV).

In Christ's Name

Love *in action* produces the fruit of faith, but *inaction* doesn't produce anything. Serving is both intentional and relational at the same time. It's more than just silently *being a Christian* and hoping those around you will be insightful enough to come to Jesus on their own. If we love people because Jesus loved us first, what's wrong with giving God credit when his love flows out through us? We've heard a lot of people say they were trying to be "silent witnesses" of God's love to those around them; but how would you feel if you asked someone to testify on your behalf in court, and they exercised their *right to remain silent* instead? Christ-like service and God-honoring words go together like macaroni and cheese—they're made for each other.

When someone close to you asks you why you're going out of your way to serve him or her, there are a lot of different ways to give God the credit. You might say something like, "It's just my small way of showing you how much God loves you." Or, "You looked like you could use some encouragement, and I thought if Jesus were here, it's what he might do." The basic message is: You're so important to God, and to me, we can't help trying to show you that every once in a while. Though it may sound a little odd the first few times it comes out of your mouth, it's something everyone needs to hear. In our experience most people—even those hostile to organized religion—appreciate the idea that God thinks they're worthy of special treatment.

Many years ago Steve tried to "win" one of his sisters to Christ by arguing with her. He'd read books on evangelism and watched others go through scripted arguments guaranteed to get anyone to "pray the prayer" of salvation. When the opportunity came during a long car ride, he was all practiced up and ready for the encounter. Through much arguing and bulldog persistence, Steve finally persuaded his sister to pray a prayer of commitment to Christ.

Unfortunately, though she'd said "all the right words," her forced conversion was neither deep nor lasting. She didn't experience any real life-change or show clear signs of the overflowing life until years later when she had a heartfelt (and non-coerced) encounter with the Lord. After that, her spiritual life really took off and she began growing like crazy.

The good news is that Steve learned from the experience. When the time came to reach out to his other sister, he took a completely fresh approach and served his way into her life instead of arguing his way in. Steve looked for dozens of little ways to pour out God's love in her presence. He gave his little sister rides without hesitation or complaining. He was openhanded when she needed money and generous with encouragement when she was down. In short, he acted like a truly loving brother and poured out the love of Jesus on his little sister. She took notice of his overflowing life and opened her heart to Jesus without a single argument or high-pressure technique. Not surprisingly, since her conversion was heartfelt and not forced, she immediately began to grow and to overflow with evidence that God was in her life.

By taking this simple, authentic approach, we appeal to those we serve. We are essentially saying, "Become friends with God; he's already a friend with you" (2 CORINTHIANS 5:20b, *The Message*).

In the same passage, the Apostle Paul calls us to be "Christ's ambassadors" and says God wants us to be the official means for communicating his message of reconciliation to all people. As his ambassadors we represent him. Our job is to act and speak in the ways he would act and speak if he were physically present with the people around us. We are to communicate and represent his living water—his unconditional love—to the world around us. Which leads us to a *very* important point. Religious people are notorious for attaching a variety of conditions to God's *unconditional* love.

No Strings Attached

If we serve in order to get something, we're really serving ourselves. Candace, a young woman we both know, related an unpleasant experience she had with some Christians who befriended her during her high school days.

> There was this group of girls in my school who all attended the same church. They seemed nice and went out of their way to talk to me and invite me to hang out after school with them. After a few weeks, they asked me to come on a weekend retreat sponsored by their church youth group. I was excited to go.
>
> It was kind of like summer camp, but a lot more religious than I was used to. On the last night, their minister got up and spoke for almost two hours about Jesus dying on the cross. His talk was filled with bloody descriptions of what the Romans did to Jesus, and how much Jesus suffered so that we could get into heaven.
>
> At the end, when the minister asked anyone who wanted to accept Jesus as their personal Savior to come up front, my friends all looked at me expectantly. I could tell they really wanted me to go forward, but something about the whole experience was just creeping me out. I could tell they were disappointed that I hadn't accepted Jesus, but I didn't realize how much.
>
> In the weeks following the retreat, my new friends seemed a lot less interested in me. When I worked up enough courage to ask one of them what I'd done to make them all mad at me, she told me it was because they didn't want to waste their time on me if I wasn't ready to get saved.
>
> I was totally humiliated when it finally dawned on me that they'd never really been my friends at all. To them I was just another prospective convert.

We wish Candace's story was unique, but unfortunately it's not. These kinds of experiences leave such a bitter taste behind, it's no surprise so many of our family members and friends have become cynical about Christians, church, and even Jesus. It's almost second nature for them to suspiciously ask, "What's the catch?" Maybe that's why in Revelation 22:17, the Spirit says, "Whoever is thirsty, let him come; and whoever wishes, let him take the free gift of the water of life" (NIV). The living water Jesus offers is an absolutely free gift—no strings attached. If we offer less, we turn God's good news into one more "bait and switch" scheme.

Once your friends and family members get past their fear of being deceived, taken advantage of, or manipulated, you'll find that their favorite F-word is "free!" That's why opportunities to serve and perform small acts of kindness that are absolutely, totally, entirely, utterly, no-kidding, no-strings-attached *free* are so powerful. When this brand of free love flows from God into you and then out to others, it's incredibly enticing to all those around you.

More Than Enough

Many of the wedding guests at Cana were probably there for the free food and free wine. And when the wine ran out, Jesus didn't just make a few glasses or a few bottles of water turn into wine. He transformed six water jars, "each holding from twenty to thirty gallons" into top-quality wine. That's somewhere between 120-180 gallons of wine—enough to fill between 600 and 800 table-sized bottles! And every drop of it was free. Nobody there earned it, and it's hard to imagine anybody at that wedding being turned away with an empty glass. It's one more picture of the amazing generosity and abundance Jesus wants to pour out to you and through you. There's more than enough of Jesus' love to overflow from you into your friends and family and into your whole community—filling everyone around you with the amazing richness and fine bouquet of his love. That's what our next section is all about.

getting your **feet wet**

Put your money where your mouth is.

Think of something you'd really like to do for yourself—like going out to a movie or buying that new fishing pole you've been eyeing down at the sporting goods store.

Now figure out how much that thing would cost and spend an equal amount on a friend or family member. Buy the person a gift that you think might communicate how important he or she is to God.

When you give your present, do it secretly, leaving a typewritten note that says something like, "Here is a small token of encouragement for you. Remember, God loves you!"

the **reflection** *pool*

>> When has someone served you in the name of Christ—no strings attached? How did that make you feel?

>> How could you transform some of your daily activities into acts of service?

>> What's one daily activity you can transform into an act of service tomorrow?

the **deep end**

FREE BBQ!

Invite at least one friend or family member over to your house for a barbecue. Or, if it's not the right season for grilling outside, host an indoor theme party and cook food from a specific region of the world. Make sure your friend or family member knows not to bring anything—this is your treat!

Serve your guests graciously and wholeheartedly as you eat, talk, play games, and enjoy one another's company.

Don't try to push the conversation toward spiritual topics—that's not the point of the evening. But do practice some of what you learned this week in the *Outflow* readings: listen actively, ask good questions, show empathy as you celebrate or mourn with your friend, pray throughout the evening for your friend, and—above all—show love to your friend.

If you're going through *Outflow* with a small group, host the barbecue dinner as a small group. Each member should invite one or more guests. Be sure you plan fun activities for your time together: conversation starters, games, and good music!

Follow up after the barbecue and let your friend or family member know what a good time you had together. Plan another opportunity to get together in the near future.

group
discussion questions

*Use these questions during your small group time and dia-
logue together about the third week of Outflow readings.*

>> In Reading 11, the book talks about "flinging seeds
of Jesus' love" as a good metaphor for sharing
Jesus with your friends and family. How might this
perspective change the way you share Jesus with the
people you love?

>> Who do you find it hardest to really listen to? How
can you practice sincerely listening to that person—
as Reading 12 described listening?

>> Think of a negative and a positive experience
you've had with Christians—how did those two
interactions affect your perception of Jesus and the
church? How can you use that experience to change
the way you share Jesus with friends and family?

>> Who else in your friends' and family members' lives
are sharing Jesus with them? How can you support
and encourage those Christians as they reach out to
your loved ones?

>> When has someone served you in the name of
Christ—no strings attached? How did that make you
feel? How can you do something similar with your
friends and family?

{ WEEK **4** }

you

your family
& friends

your
community

outward toward your community

"FOR YOU HAVE BEEN CALLED TO LIVE IN FREEDOM, MY BROTHERS AND SISTERS. BUT DON'T USE YOUR FREEDOM TO SATISFY YOUR SINFUL NATURE. INSTEAD, USE YOUR FREEDOM TO SERVE ONE ANOTHER IN LOVE. FOR THE WHOLE LAW CAN BE SUMMED UP IN THIS ONE COMMAND: 'LOVE YOUR NEIGHBOR AS YOURSELF.' "

—GALATIANS 5:13-14

"The love of our neighbor is the
only door out of the dungeon of self."

—George MacDonald

READING 16

samaria

The third tier of your life's fountain is the community that surrounds you—your neighborhood, town, city, the people who live next door, those who live on the other side of the tracks, the people who work at your local hardware or grocery store, and those who labor in the high-rise buildings downtown.

But, if like so many people, you see your community as a sea of souls and your personal influence as a tiny eyedropper, it's easy to get overwhelmed. After all, what difference can one, or 10, or even 10,000 eyedroppers of love have on the vast sea of hurting humanity around you? Yet, just as the largest ocean is made up of individual drops of water, your community is made of individual lives that need Christ's love—each one, one at a time.

A few years back, Steve traveled across the Atlantic to Brighton, England in order to equip a large group of young, 20-something Christians to influence their community. These young Brits weren't just eager to *hear* how to change their city, they wanted to go out and really get their hands dirty doing it. Here's how Steve describes what happened:

> After a couple of days explaining biblical concepts, we took up an offering to fund our outreaches in Brighton. We received something in the range of 2,000 pounds—enough to give about 20 pounds (around $35) to each group of four people. Instead of being an "ugly American" and suggesting what types of outreach were right for England, I let the crowd shout out ideas they thought would work in their city. I simply wrote down the ideas as they came in without judging their wisdom or probability of success.
>
> The ideas were all over the map! Some seemed wonderful and some sounded shockingly goofy to me as a Yank—but I held my tongue. Some of the ideas were what you might expect, and others were...um...

a bit more original, like buying "crisps" (aka potato chips) and giving them away for free to folks drinking beer in pubs. The crowd was pretty excited about this idea, as it's almost unheard of to drink beer in Brighton without a bag of crisps in your hand.

Another bold suggestion was buying cigarettes and giving them away to street people. I have to admit this one threw me, until later that night when a good number of street people showed up at our evening worship celebration. One ragged old gentleman's testimony was classic, "All right, this is my kind of church—the kind that gives out free cigarettes!"

Some of the street people brought their dogs to church with them, explaining that the dogs were their only friends in the whole world. Suddenly, God's love had become real in a way these poor and friendless people could understand. I'm not suggesting giving out free cigarettes as a regular outreach, but it sure warmed my heart to see smoking actually bringing people to church instead of keeping them away.

The same group that gave out the smokes also cleaned up garbage and broken glass in front of several shops. The shopkeepers were blown away by this small measure of kindness. Some of the most grateful shop owners were Islamic immigrants who asked a lot of questions about Jesus. Other Brighton residents had all their fines for overdue books paid at the library or received free stamps on all their letters at the post office—all so they could see God's love in a practical way.

My whole time in Brighton was just a profoundly moving time. Many people experienced the work of Jesus like never before. Even more than that—for one night at least—many who had decided Christianity was not for them were seeing Christ and his followers in a fresh new way.

The simple acts of kindness these groups of young British Christians poured out over the city were like "drops in the ocean." And yet they touched and transformed thousands of hearts. For some the changes were profound, and for others relatively small. The only sad thing about this story is that what happened in Brighton is not a normal, everyday event in every city where Christ's followers are to be found.

But we can change all that!

The "Old Normal" and the "New Normal"

It's a good bet that the perception of Christianity many people in your own community have is something less than completely positive. They've seen local priests and well-known church leaders busted in sex scandals. They've watched the lavish lifestyles of flamboyant preachers exposed on TV news shows. Worst of all, they've had personal run-ins with annoying, judgmental, and hypocritical Christians. It might have been somebody screaming at them through a bullhorn about burning in hell; or maybe a religious parent or relative who talked the Christian talk but walked a harsh and self-centered walk; or perhaps they've run into political activists who think anyone who believes in Jesus has to be part of the "religious right." Whatever the reason, many people have a bad taste in their mouths when it comes to Christianity.

It's discouraging to think about sharing Jesus with the people in your community when you know you're likely to face negative perceptions and even ugly prejudices. That's probably the reason it's become "normal" for so many who love Jesus to be afraid of openly acknowledging him out in their communities. Obviously, silence and inaction do nothing to change anyone's negative perceptions of Christianity; the only thing that can change those perceptions is for people to personally *experience* Christ's love first hand.

Perhaps that's why the two greatest commandments Jesus gave us are both about *love*. In Matthew 22:37-40, Jesus says, " 'You must *love* the Lord your God with all your heart, all your soul, and all your mind.' This is the first and greatest commandment. A second is equally important: '*Love* your neighbor as yourself.' The entire law and all the demands of the prophets are based on these two commandments" (emphasis added).

You've heard these verses before, but what would happen if you really embraced these two kinds of love as your *new normal*? What if you started loving God so much that you let what he feels for the people in your community begin to overflow into your heart? What if—as you walked through your neighborhood, grocery store, and local mall—you watched the people around you and literally ached with love for them? What if every time you looked at the people in your community, you longed for them to personally know Jesus?

What if you loved God so much that instead of being content with praying, "Thy will be done," you were always on the lookout for tangible ways to put his will into action "in earth as it is in heaven" (MATTHEW 6:10, KJV). What if you focused on dreaming up ways to let God's love flow out from you in all sorts of fun and creative actions? As you went about your daily business in the city or town where you live, what if it was normal for you to be intentionally pouring out generous words and kind actions on your neighbors? And what if you were doing all of that in Christ's name?

Wouldn't that be something?

If you set out to touch one or two people a day with some small act of kindness in the name of Jesus, every week you'd be helping to change the way between seven and 14 individuals perceive the Lord and his followers! And if you did this every week for a year, that would be somewhere between 365 and 730 acts of love in Christ's name. Even if you missed a few days here and there, you'd overflow God's love into the lives of hundreds of people—each individual little kindness a surprise package that simply and profoundly says, "You really are important to God."

We're not talking about some program that you give "the old college try" for a few days or weeks. This overflowing lifestyle of love is meant to become part of who you are for the rest of your life. Instead of just doing outreach as a project, you'll *constantly* be filling up with the joy of Jesus and *constantly* giving it away. When you tap into God's generosity and habitually pour it out in your community, you'll experience little miracles all the time. What happened in Brighton (homeless people joyfully showing up at church to express their gratitude, Muslim shopkeepers spontaneously asking questions about Jesus, and all the rest) was just the tip of the iceberg. When you get in the habit of letting God's love flow outward from you, wonders like these—and even better—will start to become part of your everyday experience.

These experiences will have a dramatic impact on the people around you, but they will have an even more powerful impact on *the person you are inside*. With each outward-focused act, you'll become a little more generous, a little more grace-giving, and a little more comfortable with pouring out Jesus' love on those you meet. The person you are—and the person others see when they meet you—will become a little more Christ-like. It's what the Apostle Paul was talking about in 2 Corinthians 3:18 when he says that our faces will begin to "reflect the Lord's glory," as we're "being transformed into his likeness with ever-increasing glory" (NIV).

This exciting new normal will not come about effortlessly or in short order. In over 20 years of trying to live it ourselves and help others get started, we've seen how strong is the human tendency toward selfishness. We've all spent so much time "looking out for number one" and "being as good as the next guy" that it's hard to break the habit. It takes time to switch from grudgingly doing the minimum amount God lets you get away with to becoming available to God every day. In fact, it's a life's work. There will always be tension between human self-focus and the outward-focused life God desires for us. That's why Jesus tells us in Matthew 6:32-33 not to worry so much about food and material possessions. "For the pagans run after all these things, and your heavenly Father knows that you need them. But seek first his kingdom and his righteousness, and all these things will be given to you as well" (NIV).

Seeking God's kingdom first means the main event of your life is focusing on God and what God focuses on: people. It means being outward toward others in the righteous, generous ways God desires. While others may devote their waking hours to bringing home the bacon or pursuing self-gratification, when you seek God's kingdom first, you're trusting in his generosity toward you *at the same time as you're sharing it with others*. It isn't that you don't go to work, go shopping, go golfing, or enjoy the hobbies that you love. It's that your life isn't *about* those things. It's making sure those things are not your life goal; but instead making your life's goal to personally grow closer to Jesus and to touch every single person you can with Christ's love. By giving away precious time, energy, and money with no expectation of getting anything in return (from people, anyway), you become "Exhibit A" testifying that God's promises are the real deal. And, as we've said again and again, it's not like you'll run out of what you need. The verse says specifically that if we seek God's kingdom first, he'll provide us with all those other things that we need. God loves us! And if we're being generous toward him, is God really going to be anything less toward us? Of course not! Walking by faith in God's generosity may sound like a hardship to those who don't yet trust him, but after you've been doing it a while, it's so exciting it's addictive.

The new normal of God's kingdom—this overflowing generosity—is much more fun and satisfying than the world's old normal of fear and selfishness. Make no mistake about it—there's no comparison between the kinds of outreach we're talking about and nervously handing out pamphlets that say, "God loves you" with a few Bible verses attached. The new normal is overflowing with Jesus-style encounters any of us can experience for ourselves. And in most cases the recipients of the overflowing kindness we're talking about are much more grateful than anyone who gets a Bible tract. It's sort of like being inside the New Testament experiencing Jesus' love, witnessing the abundant joy and generosity in the early church believers, and seeing more and more people coming to know Jesus personally.

More Than Just You

Imagine if a church of 250 members adopted this generous new norm and every single person made a commitment to reach one or two people a day with Jesus' love.

Just imagine! That church would touch between 1,700 and 3,500 people *per week*! And the things they'd be doing would be so full of genuine caring that those who received them wouldn't quickly forget—people remember acts of kindness for days, weeks, and in our experience, even years! Now multiply that impact by a month of just four weeks—that's between 6,800 and 14,000 drops of love raining down on your city! Sometimes one of those drops will lead to a conversation; sometimes it'll just bring a smile. But all the while, each of those encounters will quietly slide someone a little further toward God.

Fast forward. In a year's time these little encounters would add up to between 88,400 and 182,000 drops of love in the "sea" of your city—all of that coming out of a church of just 250.

Of course if your church were embracing this new normal, it wouldn't stay at 250 members for long! Those little drops of love would fall into all kinds of lives, and some of them would land in hearts ready to seek Jesus. Your church and many others would begin to see a whole new group of people seeking, finding, and beginning to follow Jesus. Your life and the lives of all the others in your growing church would begin overflowing with rich experiences and inspiring true stories that would draw more people like magnets.

We hope you're inspired by this vision of everyday people constantly overflowing with life and reaching out with loving actions. We'd like to see it sweep across our nation and the world to replace some of the self-focused stuff that goes on now in many churches. To us, this vision sounds like what Jesus had in mind in Matthew 28:19-20 when he said, "Therefore, go and make disciples of all nations, baptizing them in the name of the Father and the Son and the Holy Spirit. Teach these new disciples to obey all the commands I have given you. And be sure of this: I am with you always, even to the end of the age" (MATTHEW 28:19-20). As far as we can tell, *every* single disciple of Christ is meant to be part of the "going" and "baptizing" and "teaching," not just the highly skilled or talkative few. Extroverts or introverts, shy or outgoing, it doesn't matter. It's a big world, and if each of us pours out our little eyedropper-full of Christ into one or two lives everyday, God can use us to bring about tremendous change in our communities. And in the process, God will change us to be more and more like Jesus!

Though it may not seem like you can make much of a difference, God has entrusted you with the power to give thousands a taste of Jesus and awaken their thirst. In the process, you'll help change the way an amazing number of people in your community think and feel about Jesus and his followers. So let's give our all—heart, soul, mind, and strength—as we invest in something that lasts forever, the people Jesus loves and died for. It'll be fun. We promise.

getting your **feet wet**

Pull your community's phone book out of the drawer. As you flip through it, think about some of the negative perceptions the people listed might have about Jesus and his followers. Write them in the space provided.

....

....

....

....

....

....

....

....

....

....

....

Once you've written down a few negative perceptions, think of some possible actions that might counteract those perceptions. If you're really feeling inspired, go out and try a few of your ideas in the community!

the **reflection** *pool*

>>What comes to mind when you think of ways you can personally overflow Jesus' love into your community?

>>What was your "old normal" attitude? How is that different from the "new normal" described in today's reading?

>>How can you move from one attitude to the other?

> "THEREFORE CONSIDER
> CAREFULLY HOW YOU LISTEN.
> WHOEVER HAS WILL BE
> GIVEN MORE; WHOEVER DOES
> NOT HAVE, EVEN WHAT HE
> THINKS HE HAS WILL BE
> TAKEN FROM HIM."
>
> **—LUKE 8:18** (NIV)

> "One of the best ways to persuade
> anyone is with your ears—by
> listening to them."
>
> —Dean Rusk,
> Former U.S. Secretary of State

READING 17

listening to strangers

Much to the chagrin of many of the people at her conservative home church, Carol, a 25-year-old Bible college graduate, took a job as a server at a trendy nightclub. A month later, she ran into the leader of her mother's Bible study at the grocery store. After greeting Carol, the older woman drew her close and with a look of deep concern said, "I've been praying for you ever since your mother told me where you're working. *How are you doing?*"

Carol smiled and answered truthfully, "I guess your prayers are being answered. In the four weeks I've been working at the club, I've led three people into relationship with Jesus. How are you doing?"

Carol's success in reaching out at the club is worth a second look. In one month she introduced more than three times the number of people to Christ than half the churches in North America do in a whole year. Surprisingly, Carol explains her outreach efforts didn't depend as much on the *location* of where she worked as they did on another frequently overlooked "L-word"— *Listening*.

What Carol discovered while working at the club is that many people who'd normally recoil at religious sounding words are more than ready to open up to someone—even a total stranger—who cares enough to genuinely listen. Reaching out with Jesus' love to the strangers in your community and *listening* to them go together like peanut butter and jelly. They're the perfect combination! Those little acts of love and kindness may open a door to relationship, but effective listening allows you to step through that door.

Some people confuse the admonition in James 1:19 to be "quick to listen" with being passive about your faith. But nothing could be further from the truth. "Servant listening" is one of the most vigorous and proactive behaviors you can ever engage in. This type of listening requires you to be much more conscious and alert in your day-to-day activities and conversations than most people.

Listen With Your Eyes

Part of letting God's love flow from you to your community is becoming a people-watcher and a mood-noticer. As you pass people on the street or see them sitting near you in a restaurant, take notice of the smiles or frowns on their faces. Pay attention to the feelings they're communicating through posture, body language, and facial expressions. Such seemingly minor nuances speak volumes about what's going on in people's hearts. No, you're not being a busybody; you're practicing *the ministry of noticing*. Paying attention to strangers helps you begin looking outside of yourself and start genuinely caring about people. And as you begin to notice people, soon you may find yourself talking to God about those people—praying that they might have a better day, or asking God to give them peace in the midst of what seems like a hectic schedule. And sometimes you'll even be moved to risk personally reaching out.

Here's a story that a buddy of ours told us recently. He and a couple of friends were eating lunch together at their local Cracker Barrel restaurant when they noticed the lady sitting next to them.

> As we ate I noticed something sad about this woman's eyes. While my friends talked, I prayed a little silent prayer for her and immediately got the impression that maybe I was supposed to buy her lunch. So I grabbed her bill off the table and said, "You look like you could use a little encouragement today. Let me pay for your lunch."
>
> She smiled and said, "Thank you very much," and went about finishing her meal as if nothing particularly interesting had happened.
>
> As she rose to leave, she paused uneasily at our table and then said, "I really did need some encouragement today." Then she sat down with us and began crying. She told us about her son who had recently died very tragically. "I have good days and bad days," she said, "And today was a *really* bad day—until you came along."
>
> We listened for a while longer as she told more of her story. And eventually I asked if we could pray with her. She took our hands and prayed with us right there in the Cracker Barrel. More tears came, but instead of looking sad, now she was smiling thoughtfully. At last, she looked up and said, "I knew there was something special about you guys when you first walked through the door. Thank you again!"
>
> Looking back on that day, I hope what she sensed as we walked in the door was Jesus noticing her. I'm realizing more and more what a holy thing it is to notice people—especially the ones who are the least noticeable.

Noticing and listening to the people in your community are extraordinarily powerful ways of showing God's love. Unfortunately, genuinely caring listeners always seem to be in short supply.

The truth is, there are opportunities to listen with your eyes and ears every place you go—even when you're not in the mood. Recently Dave was stuck at O'Hare International Airport in Chicago for over eight hours as he tried to catch a two-hour flight a few days before the New Year. An unofficial labor slowdown had snarled air traffic—and travelers' moods all over the country.

After watching helplessly as two of my flights were cancelled, and the newest one postponed several times, I was in a terrible mood. With the exception of lacking smoldering torches, my fellow passengers were beginning to look like irate villagers getting ready to storm the gates of Dr. Frankenstein's castle. OK, maybe I have a slightly overactive imagination, but if the loudspeaker announced one more delay or gate change, I was ready to find a torch and lead the abused masses in storming Gate E-29!

But then I sensed God's still, small voice trying to break through my indignation with a thought totally opposite of the violent scene I was imagining in my head. The voice said, "Dave, you can either be miserable like everyone else, or you can be my light in this darkness. You've written books on kindness and listening...this would be a good time to practice what you preach."

A smile spread across my face and my spirit immediately lifted. I realized I wasn't trapped in the airport at all (or a scary movie for that matter). I was in the perfect place to let Christ's light shine.

So I closed my laptop and began looking around for someone to serve. The people sitting near me looked bored, so I gathered up newspapers others had cast aside, put them back together and walked around asking people if they'd like one. Even people who'd already read the paper appreciated the offer and took my little gesture as an invitation to connect. When they asked why I was handing out "recycled" papers, I said I thought God would rather have me doing something positive than sitting around feeling sorry for myself. Though I got one or two puzzled looks, most people seemed to applaud my behavior. Some even offered to let me distribute their used magazines and the paperbacks they'd finished.

I'm not particularly extroverted, but I have to admit I was really beginning to have fun being "God's newspaper boy." Instead of a time of suffering, God transformed the hours I spent at the airport that day into some of the most enjoyable and fruitful times of connecting I've ever had. Several of the people welcomed my offer of a newspaper or a book as an opportunity to talk to a friendly person. I was amazed how many complete strangers wanted to talk and how open they were when they did.

One young man in particular was a backup musician for a well-known pop star. As we talked he told me how much he missed the connection with God he'd known growing up in a close-knit, Christian family. He confessed, "When my career went on the front burner, there just wasn't any room for Jesus...but talking to you, makes me remember what I'm missing." Then he asked if I knew of any good churches in the city where he lived when he wasn't on tour. I mentioned a couple of possibilities and gave him my e-mail address so he could tell me how it went. We were having such a good conversation that I found myself extremely disappointed when my flight was finally called and I had to board my plane. Two weeks later I got an e-mail thanking me for helping him get back in church and get "right with God."

I didn't do much more than listen to him and the other people I connected with that day, but somehow God showed up. In just about every conversation, it felt like folks saw me as a representative of a God who wanted to do good things for them. In fact, it was such an encouraging experience that I was reminded of this verse in the book of Hebrews, "Don't forget to show hospitality to strangers, for some who have done this have entertained angels without realizing it!" (HEBREWS 13:2). Whether there were angels there or not, that day in the airport has forever changed how I view the "inconvenience" of travel delays and flight cancellations.

Many situations we perceive as inconveniences are actually spiritual opportunities in disguise. In fact we're pretty sure there are exciting divine appointments all around us most of the time. They're just waiting to happen when we're willing to listen to God and pay attention to the people around us. If you're having a hard time imagining yourself praying for someone sitting next to you at the Cracker Barrel or handing out newspapers in the airport, don't worry. There are plenty of remarkably fun and effective ways to notice and let God's love flow out from you to others—without making much noise at all.

Go and Listen

After surviving Hurricane Katrina and days of waiting for rescue on roof-tops and highway overpasses, more than 30,000 refugees found temporary shelter in the Astrodome and the Reliant Arena in Houston, Texas. A crowd of over 1,000 willing volunteers from all over Houston and around the nation gathered to do all they could to help. Many were doctors, nurses, and experienced disaster relief workers, but many others were ordinary followers of Jesus willing to do anything to help the people of the temporary city. Dave and his wife, Pam, were part of this latter group.

> As we looked out over the sea of stunned refugees in front of us, we were trying to imagine how in the world God could possibly use us to make a real difference. When we were praying back home in Cincinnati, we'd been so sure the Holy Spirit wanted us to drop everything, get on a plane, and come to Houston to help—but how? The only answer we got consisted of two words: *go* and *listen*.

When Pam and I first arrived, we let the people in charge know we were willing to do anything. And they took us up on it. My first job was helping nurses remove urine-soaked clothing from completely terrified male Alzheimer's patients. Though they didn't understand where they were or what was going on, they all wanted to know someone was listening to them. The more we listened and restated what they said—to show we were trying to understand—the calmer and more willing they were to let us help them.

Once everyone was happily clothed in fresh, clean garments, my wife and I asked our supervisor what other things we could do. He thought for a minute and said, "Just go out among the cots and listen to people's stories. They've been through a lot, and they need to talk about it."

With no more specific instructions than these, we waded out into the cots and began connecting with people. Almost before we could ask where people were from, they were pouring out story after story of loss and tragedy. They talked about how they'd survived and what they would do now—and invariably they asked what brought us all the way from Cincinnati to Houston. We simply said that we thought God wanted us to come and listen to people. When we said this, people almost always asked if we would pray for them, so we did. Over and over again, we listened and they asked us to pray. It was amazing; the idea that we would come just to listen opened spiritual doors like nothing I've ever seen. These people were so hungry to be heard and so hungry to pray that after a few hours we were nearly worn out.

On the way out of the building we spotted a huge banner hanging in a prime location near the central lobby. The banner read, "Prayer." Beneath the banner there was one older man sitting all by himself. When we asked how "the prayer business" was going, he told us he was deeply disappointed because only a handful of the people in the arena wanted prayer.

"No way!" we said and explained how we'd spent hours swamped with people hungry to be listened to and prayed for. We suggested that he get out of his booth and go out among the people to listen to them. Over the next few days, every time we passed that big prayer banner, we rejoiced to see the chair under it sitting empty. You see, instead of hanging around waiting for people to come to him seeking prayer, our friend had gone on a *listening expedition.*

If God has two words for anybody who wants to overflow with love, we think those words might be *go* and *listen*. The best way to connect with not-yet Christians isn't to stand at a safe distance under billboards announcing that God is real and that he loves them. No! We've got to *go* were they are and demonstrate that love *in person.*

Get Out There!

"Go where?" you ask. The answer is places where people are—parks, shopping malls, ballgames, concerts, and fireworks displays. Any place people hang out and have fun is usually a good place to go and show God's love.

After all, if nothing else, going to fun places and having fun will help explode the idea that Christians don't know how to have a good time.

And if you're not sure where to begin, start by "listening with your eyes." Notice what people are doing and what they're talking about. Notice if people are happy or sad. Notice when people look like they need a friend, and when people seem not to want to be bothered. Then ask God to show you practical ways to reach out in ways that address those people's needs—whether it's through prayer, engaging in conversation, showing small acts of kindness, or simply sitting down and continuing to listen.

getting your **feet wet**

Initiate a conversation with someone you don't know very well: your barber, a delivery person, neighbor, or restaurant server. Listen closely to the person. Find out about what's going on in his or her life. If the opportunity arises, ask if there is anything the person would like you to pray for. Then go home and pray. The next time you see the person, check in and see how he or she is doing and specifically ask about his or her prayer request.

the **reflection** *pool*

>> Where can you go and listen to people in your community? Once you are there, how will you listen to the people around you?

>> Does this approach to listening seem like something you can personally do for those in your community? Why or why not?

>> How does this type of listening change the way you view outreach into your community?

> "I CHOSE YOU AND
> APPOINTED YOU TO GO
> AND BEAR FRUIT—FRUIT
> THAT WILL LAST. THEN
> THE FATHER WILL GIVE
> YOU WHATEVER YOU
> ASK IN MY NAME."
>
> **—JOHN 15:16** (NIV)

> "Only a life lived for
> others is worth living."
>
> —Albert Einstein

READING 18

loving your city

Is it possible to genuinely love a whole city toward Jesus? For over 20 years we've been answering this question with an enthusiastic and resounding "Yes!" We've worked hard to come up with fresh, new ways to reach our city with Jesus' love—helping to create over 300 different kinds of "community projects" for offering "humble acts of service in Christ's name with no strings attached." And in the process, we've personally washed thousands of cars for free, distributed untold numbers of complimentary soft drinks, and even scrubbed toilets in hundreds of businesses—all to let the people in our city see that Jesus personally cares about them.

The church Steve founded in Cincinnati and its 22 daughter churches all over town are known throughout the area as "the ones that do all those generous things in the name of Jesus." People from these churches touch and serve between half-a-million and a million people every year through a variety of programs and outreach events. But as great as these projects are, Steve says participating in an outreach every now and then is *not* what God wants from you.

Jesus says, "You are my friends if you do what I command. I no longer call you slaves, because a master doesn't confide in his slaves. Now you are my friends, since I have told you everything the Father told me. You didn't choose me. I chose you. I appointed you to go and produce lasting fruit, so that the Father will give you whatever you ask for, using my name. This is my command: Love each other" (JOHN 15:14-17).

If you're a friend of Jesus, it's only natural to care about what he cares about and to want to do what he does *all the time*. The overflowing life he's calling you into is more than an occasional thing—it's daily. So whatever you do to pay your bills, it's just a means to fulfilling this higher calling. The Apostle Paul funded his day-to-day outreach by making tents, but you might fund yours by working for an insurance company or a plumbing supply business. Whatever it is that you do, you can go about your day intentionally flinging seeds, nurturing relationships, and bearing lasting fruit for God in the lives around you. If you do this, loving your city will become *part of your everyday lifestyle!*

A Countercultural Love

Loving your community to Christ means making a deeper commitment to it than most people ever do. It means putting down deep roots and really caring about the physical and spiritual welfare of everyone who lives there. It's true you're just passing through on your way to heaven, but as long as you live there, reaching the people in your city or town is part of your mission from God.

Of course, this goes against the prevailing "me first" message of our culture. The 24/7 media blitz around us keeps telling us we've got to "shop around." We get so busy hunting for the best deals and the most convenient locations that we never commit to being a part of the place where we live. We need to get involved in what's happening locally. Shop at the same stores. Eat at the same restaurants. Get to know the clerks by name. Request to sit in a certain server's section (and tip generously!). Be willing to stand in the longest checkout line in order to chat with a clerk you know. Sure, it may cost you time and a few more pennies to shop at your local grocery or eat at a local restaurant, but the opportunity to get to know people makes it more than worth it.

In fact, Steve has made it his personal mission to live this sort of lifestyle in his city.

> I've made a strategic decision to do all my shopping at the same stores over and over. I want to get to know the clerks and managers by name. I'm willing to stand in the longest checkout line if it means getting a chance to talk even briefly with a new friend I'm starting to develop a relationship with. The name of the game isn't saving 90 seconds in line, it's making *generous relational investments.* If the employee I'm hoping to see isn't there, I ask about him or her and do my best to make friends with my current teller. Often I give that person a dollar or two as a tip or a gift certificate to a carwash or something else that might demonstrate the generosity of Jesus.
>
> People love getting little gifts. And they love being recognized and treated with dignity even more. One way I know I'm making progress is when several different employees start saying, "Hi Steve!" when I pass them in the grocery store aisles or on the street. Since we're becoming friends, it's the most natural thing in the world to ask how their family is doing and if there is anything they'd like me to pray about. As they get to know me better, it's also natural for them to begin finding out about me and my church. Each week I try to go just a little deeper.
>
> It's amazing how much people will share if I slow down long enough to listen. In fact, so many people that I connect with in this way ask me for directions to my church that I've had cards printed up. The cards say, "Here's your invitation to the party!" They give my personal phone number, explain when our celebrations are, and provide directions and a map. They also explain a few distinctions that set our church apart.
>
> Although I live in a metro area with a population of well over a million, I try to live a "small town" lifestyle. I go out of my way to learn the names and histories of the people I meet. Folks who know me notice that I frequent the same small handful of restaurants all the time. It's

not just because I'm boring or even because burritos are my absolute favorite food. It's because I love my city so much that I want to get to know its people well enough to help them get to know Jesus.

There are so many practical ways to love your city...

When you go to the grocery store or to the gas station, stop and talk to the tellers. Don't scan your groceries in the self-serve line just to save a few minutes. If your gas station is one where you pay at the pump with your credit card, make up a reason to go inside the station and talk to a person. Go in there and buy a Coke or a bottle of water and talk; find out the cashier's name, and start a conversation that will continue for weeks or months. Don't be tempted to shop around. Sure, you might save a penny or two across the street, but what's the value of a few cents compared with a relationship that could impact someone's eternity? Loving your city isn't necessarily convenient, but it's rich and exciting—and totally worth it.

One thing we've discovered in 20 years of outreach is that most people really *do* want to talk when you approach them the right way. If you avoid putting the gospel cart before the relational horse that draws it, you'll go a long way. During the past several decades, people have become averse to hearing about the gospel without first seeing and experiencing the practical love of Christ in action. Though it's needed now more than ever, loving people as a means of introducing Jesus is nothing new. It's a New Testament idea that goes all the way back to Jesus himself. When Jesus proclaimed the coming kingdom, he fed and healed people, too. When the early church told others about Jesus, they also helped the poor and took care of widows. The truth of their words was validated by the power of their loving actions.

If we're followers of Jesus, pouring out his love in practical, visible ways needs to be part of our essential nature. After all, we're following the greatest, most loving person of all time. All others are mere shadows by comparison. Whether you're an extrovert or an introvert, there are plenty of ways you can pour out the love of the Master.

Quiet Approaches for Quiet People

One of Steve's best friends is the regional head of an insurance company. For years his national office used "We're the Quiet Company" as their advertising slogan. It makes sense doesn't it? Wouldn't you prefer a quiet, gentle insurance agent to one that's loud and flashy? Even though surveys have consistently shown that about 75 percent of the general population in America and Western Europe is at least slightly extroverted, in our experience most followers of Christ (and the people around them) feel more at home with calm, understated outreach.

For this reason—and because they usually listen far better than their extroverted counterparts—*introverts* are some of the most effective evangelists around. We know this sounds contrary to the image you've been led to expect, but it's true nevertheless. Small things done by quiet people can change the world. Here are two quiet and not-so-scary ways to love your community toward Jesus:

One of Steve's all-time favorites is *paying for the meal of the person behind you in line at the drive-through*. As you stop at the window to pay for your food, tell the cashier you're paying for the order behind you as well—the cashier will probably already know the total cost of that meal. Once you've paid, give the cashier a dollar tip for telling the lucky person behind you, "Someone bought your meal today as a practical way of saying God loves you." If you're too shy to say all this to the cashier, write it out on a card and ask the cashier to give it to the next customer along with the food. And don't forget that dollar tip, it will make the cashier's day!

Another idea for quietly reaching out in your community is to *be a great tipper*. Waiters and waitresses will tell you that church people (followers of the most generous person the world has ever seen) have the reputation of being the least generous tippers. You can change this by putting down a nice tip of at least 20 percent—and then adding another 5 percent or 10 percent on top of that! When your server comes to collect the check, say, "Here's a little extra something just to remind you that God loves you." Again, if you're too shy to say it, you can always write it on the check. You don't have to confine yourself to restaurants, either. Try noticing, talking to, and tipping anyone who serves you wherever you go. Give the cashier at the grocery or the attendant at the tollbooth a warm blessing along with an extra dollar or two. Learn their names and choose their lines even when others would be faster.

These people who are serving you will be awestruck as you turn around and pour out a little kindness in God's name. Be ready to answer when they ask, "Why are you so different?" or "What church do you go to?" It will happen more and more as you continue to pour out God's love in your community.

A Chosen Few

Although we want to pour out love wherever we go, it's also a good idea to consciously ask God to assign particular people to us—people whom you can really start building a relationship with. Regularly take time to pray and ask God to bring people into your life who you can love toward him.

Maybe God will give you three or four people—or even a dozen—who you're praying for and consistently reaching out to in any given month or year. Some people may tend to confuse your acts of love and generosity with flirting, and so if you're a woman, it's often wiser to focus on reaching out to women and if you're a man, reach out to men.

As you consistently show practical love, mercy, and generosity week after week, you'll draw that person closer and closer to a place where it's natural to invite him or her to "God's party!" This might mean inviting that person to catch lunch or a movie with you and some friends at your home, or inviting your friend to a Sunday worship celebration or some other activity at your church. Unfortunately over the years we've found that one of the main reasons people don't come to church is that *nobody has ever invited them*! But it's really not that hard—if you have a relationship established first, it's rarely an offensive gesture to invite someone to church.

Just say something like, "Hey, since we're getting to know one another better, I'd like to invite you to come with me to…" Then enthusiastically describe what you have in mind. If it's lunch, and you love Chipotle as much as Steve does, you might say, "I want to buy you a burrito as big as your head and hear more of your story!" If it's a church activity, describe what will happen in accurate, positive ways—but keep it short and upbeat. Oh, and it never hurts to say, "Afterward, I want to take you out to eat."

And, if you're worried that once people know you're a Christian they'll start asking tough questions about your faith, don't fear! We've done this hundreds of times and nobody has ever asked one of those complicated theo-logical questions we thought we were supposed to have answers for. As we mentioned in the last chapter, listening is usually more powerful than talk-ing. If you give them the opportunity, most people love talking about them-selves. If they talk about faith at all, usually it's to ask you about your story. When they do, don't give them the super-extended version; keep it brief and they'll ask for more if they want to hear it. Don't worry about quoting Bible verses or offering long-winded theological treatises. In our experience, when people ask about the Bible it will probably be something like, "What kind of Bible should I read?" Our answer is: "Whichever one you want, just make sure it's easy to understand!"

If you ask God for them, you'll get lots of opportunities to invite people to check out your small group or church and—even more importantly—to turn complete strangers into your friends and eventually into friends of Jesus. As you go around your community pouring out Jesus' love—doing all kinds of good to all kinds of people all the time, the word will get out. People will begin to tilt their heads and ask, "What has gotten into you?" Then you can just smile and thank God that *he* is not only getting into you, he's getting out in ways that change everything!

getting your **feet wet**

Write down some of the places you go during your average week. Where do you buy your food or put gasoline in your car? What restaurants are your favorites?

....

....

....

....

Now think about some practical ways you could pour Jesus' love out to the people in these places. Write some of your ideas in the space below and pick one to try this week.

the **reflection** pool

>> What places in your community do you already go to on a regular basis? How can you connect with the people in those places?

>> Who in your community has God placed in your life so that you can reach that person—or people—with his love?

>> Specifically, how can you personally make a commitment of love to your city?

> "WHEN YOU GIVE A
> LUNCHEON OR DINNER,
> DO NOT INVITE YOUR
> FRIENDS, YOUR BROTHERS
> OR RELATIVES, OR YOUR RICH
> NEIGHBORS; IF YOU DO, THEY
> MAY INVITE YOU BACK AND
> SO YOU WILL BE REPAID. BUT
> WHEN YOU GIVE A BANQUET,
> INVITE THE POOR, THE
> CRIPPLED, THE LAME,
> THE BLIND, AND YOU
> WILL BE BLESSED."
>
> **—LUKE 14:12-14** (NIV)

> "What I must do is all
> that concerns me,
> not what other people think."
>
> —Ralph Waldo Emerson

READING 19

share the party

First, Break All the Rules

While Jesus was on earth, he attended a fancy Sabbath meal in the home of one of the most prominent religious leaders in Jerusalem at that time. Before he sat down at the table, Jesus livened up that stuffy old dinner party in a rather dramatic way. He reached out his hand and healed a man suffering from a painful swelling of the extremities—something that's often a sign of congestive heart failure. But instead of rejoicing for the man whose life had probably just been saved, the guests were scandalized. In their eyes, by curing this man on the Sabbath, Jesus was breaking all the rules.

It's clear that Jesus didn't mind flouting social and religious conventions if that's what it took to show God's love to someone who really needed it. Rumors about how the controversial carpenter from Nazareth had hugged lepers, eaten with tax gatherers, and conversed with "scarlet women" had no doubt already given Jesus a bad reputation among these "righteous" leaders. But it's one thing to hear about such politically incorrect behavior and quite another to see it in action. Luke 14:4-6 gives the impression that everybody at the party stood by speechless and uncomfortable when Jesus asked, "Is it permitted in the law to heal people on the Sabbath day, or not?" and then, "Which of you doesn't work on the Sabbath? If your son or your cow falls into a pit, don't you rush to get him out?"

They all knew the obvious answer. Of course saving a person's life—or even an animal's—was more important than meticulously observing the Sabbath regulations. But not one of these "righteous" men would risk speaking up. Our guess is they were worried about their reputations and they knew that agreeing with Jesus while in attendance at this particular party would negatively affect their status. They'd spent years climbing the social ladder and working to be included as part of the "in-crowd" invited to this party. None of them were about to blow it now. That's just the kind of high-pressure, no-fun dinner party it was.

Jesus understood all of this, but he didn't go along with it. So he cheerfully broke one more social rule by announcing the following to his host and fellow guests:

"When you put on a luncheon or a banquet," he said, "don't invite your friends, brothers, relatives, and rich neighbors. For they will invite you back, and that will be your only reward. Instead, invite the poor, the crippled, the lame, and the blind. Then at the resurrection of the righteous, God will reward you for inviting those who could not repay you" (LUKE 14:12-14).

In other words, if you really want to have a great time, don't go about building up your reputation by inviting the city's most famous and successful "movers and shakers." Build your connection with God by inviting the people he loves and your city would rather forget.

That's what Angie and her children did after she helped cook lunch for one of our Servant Evangelism workshops in an upscale suburban church. When an unexpected heavy snowfall cut attendance at the workshop by half, there were huge amounts of homemade vegetable soup and lots of first-rate deli sandwiches left over. Inspired by all the teaching about God's kindness (and realizing her five children would never eat *vegetable* soup); Angie decided to take the extra food downtown and give it away to the homeless.

Angie didn't really even know where to begin looking for homeless people. So she just drove down into the core of the city and told her kids to keep their eyes open for anyone who looked hungry. By the time they got downtown it was 8:30 at night, dark, and temperatures had fallen below zero. Angie drove around until one of her kids pointed out a man warming his hands over a tiny fire in the parking lot of an abandoned gas station. Angie pulled up and offered him some hot soup and sandwiches. He accepted and as he finished eating, Angie asked if he knew anyone else who might like some hot food. When they found some of his friends, Angie ladled out bowls of steaming soup and her kids distributed sandwiches and cookies. After a while ragged men began materializing from hiding places somewhere out in the freezing darkness—each one eager for some hot soup and encouraging words. It was nothing like Angie had expected, but it was truly amazing nevertheless.

On their way home, using a word he'd only recently learned from reading the book *Charlotte's Web*, Angie's son said, "Mom, when you were feeding those homeless men you were *radiant!*"

This would've been an inspiring story if it ended here, but it isn't nearly over. Angie, her husband Tom, and her kids were so moved by what they'd experienced, they gathered friends and neighbors from three different churches and started coming downtown on a regular basis to share food and listening ears with the street people who lived there. They even sponsored a citywide "banquet for the homeless" inspired by the words of Christ we read earlier. Angie phoned the local transit authority and persuaded them to provide free bus transportation to any homeless person who wanted to come. That night, over 460 street people attended a wonderful buffet meal served on fine linen tablecloths with centerpieces of fresh cut flowers.

At each place setting, Angie and her friends placed a white stone with a Bible verse inscribed on it to remind each guest how important he or she is to God. After dinner, one of the homeless men stood up and announced, "I'm not going to be homeless forever." Holding up his white stone for everyone to see, he continued, "Someday I'm going to have a house with a mantle...and that's where I'm going to put this stone that says God loves me. You know, before today, I was planning to kill myself. I didn't see any hope...but now...now I want to live again!"

A series of healings had begun in the moment Angie told her kids, "Get in the car, we're going downtown to feed the homeless." Now doctors and dentists from all over town were coming to offer free medical services and churches were mobilizing to provide long-term food and shelter ministries that continue to this day. It's amazing how many good things were set in motion when Angie obeyed what seemed like a passing generous impulse. Angie sums up the experience saying, "It was a time of God working one miracle after another in the most practical way."

But as far as we're concerned, one of the best parts of the story came a month or two after the banquet when Angie asked her daughter Bethany how she'd like to celebrate her eighth birthday. Without any hesitation the little girl pleaded excitedly, "Can I bring my school friends to have ice cream and cupcakes with our homeless friends downtown?"

So that week after Bethany and her friends fed the homeless from the back of the family minivan, Bethany gave out birthday cupcakes. Even though some of the men sang happy birthday and gave her best wishes, the conversation wasn't exactly what you'd expect at a "normal party." As the singing and cupcake eating was going on, Angie and Tom were busy listening to one of the guys explain that his arm was bandaged because it had been chewed by a rat while he was passed out drunk.

It may sound a little crazy, but we think that's exactly the kind of people and the kind of party Jesus had in mind!

Everyone's Invited!

Each time you go out and share an act of service, each time you show generosity in the spirit of Christ, you're inviting others to come to God's "party." Unfortunately, the "celebrations" many churches are throwing *feel more like funerals*. Like the Pharisee's party that Jesus attended; unspoken rules, dead-boring religious traditions, and an endless, unceasing torrent of words take center stage in these places. That's something Christ's followers need to rise up and change right now. Stop the funerals—start the party! Jesus' party is all about letting his love overflow in ways that are authentic and fresh. It's about putting generosity and faith into action instead of talking people to death. It's about reaching out and building bridges to struggling people and helping them overcome real problems. Most of all, it's about inviting every person who God loves, in such a way that says, "Whoever you are and whatever you've done, you're welcome at Jesus' party!"

Because Jesus wasn't just talking about inviting the homeless people of your city to his banquet—Jesus wants you to seek *everyone* the upright Pharisees of the world are uncomfortable or embarrassed to have at "their" party.

> With this in mind, a small group of men and women we know recently went to eat at a nearby Hooters nightclub. If you aren't familiar with Hooters, it's famous for its pretty, young serving girls dressed in very tight-fitting T-shirts and short shorts. And you could say its mostly male clientele is usually more interested in the "scenery" than the food.
> But the small group didn't go to ogle the girls. They went to invite the Hooters waitresses and other employees to Christ's party—because they knew no one else would.
>
> They'd prepared about a dozen gift bags and filled the bags with pieces of gourmet candy, granola bars, a bottle of water and other little things the servers and the people back in the kitchen might appreciate. As the small group ordered food and drinks, they struck up a friendly conversation with Cindy, their server, and then proceeded to go about eating and enjoying each other's company. When Cindy came back with their check, all the pretty gift bags were sitting on the table.

"Is it somebody's birthday?" she asked.

"No," one of the group members said, "They're for you and the other people who work here."

"Why would you want to do that?" Cindy asked in amazement.

A group member happily chimed in saying, "These bags are just our little way of saying that God really loves you!"

Flustered, Cindy said, "Wait a minute; I'm going to get the manager."

A tense moment passed before Cindy returned with an anxious looking restaurant manager in tow. "Tell him what you told me!" Cindy said.

"We wanted to tell you how impressed we are by the service we've been getting all night," one of the group members said. "Cindy and the other young women here are doing a great job."

The manager was looking a little confused as Cindy pointed to the gift bags on the table and said, "They brought us these gifts to let us know God loves us! Is it OK for the others to come get their presents?"

A relieved look spread over the manger's face. "I can't see why not," he drawled. "Just bring 'em out here one at a time."

As Cindy rushed back into the kitchen to tell her friends to come get their presents, the manager said, "When she told me there was a group of Christians out here who wanted to ask me a question, I don't know what I was expecting. But you guys are welcome here any time."

As each employee came out to pick up a gift bag, he or she asked something like, "Tell me again why you are doing this!" or "What's the name of your church and what time do you meet?" They were all curious about the kind of church that cared more about loving people than judging them for working at Hooters.

This story happened a few weeks before we wrote this, so we don't know if any of those who received a gift bag and an invitation to "Christ's party" will show up at church. But we've seen what can happen plenty of times.

When you consistently go out into your city sharing God's love with no strings attached, lots of people start checking out your church or small group. Here's the hitch: If you throw a party, you've got to be ready for everyone who shows up. Let's say that again: *everyone*.

Get Ready...Here They Come!

We've trained lots of people to do this "inviting thing" over the years. In several dozen cases it worked so well that the overall character of the inviting congregations started to change in a big way. Lots of new faces began showing up—lots of *different* faces. At first the folks who held the purse strings would say, "Of course we want to reach *those* people. Praise God! We'll welcome them all!" But as more folks who didn't dress, or talk, or believe like them started walking through their doors, guess what happened? That's right, they quietly tracked down the "culprits" responsible for all of this disruptive growth and ordered them to make it stop. In many cases, staff members who'd dramatically increased their church attendance were fired. Really. It's happened time and time again.

It's difficult to admit, but there's a little *Pharisee* in all of us. Like the Pharisees, if you're willing to reach out at all, you'd probably rather go to friends, relatives, or neighbors who automatically recognize and obey your particular social, racial, or economic group's unspoken rules. But if you want to experience the overflowing power of Christ's kingdom on earth, you've got to reach out to the people who don't know or care about *your* rules. Instead of seeking out those who might do you some good, or donate to your church, or make you look good; Jesus commands you to go love and serve those who can never repay you.

Inviting the poor, the crippled, the sick, and other socially ostracized people is just about guaranteed to make the hidden Pharisee in you uncomfortable—in a way Jesus really likes. If you'll allow it to, it will help you humbly acknowledge your own prejudices, brokenness, and blindness. Soon there will be no room for feeling superior or inferior, but there will be plenty of opportunities for Jesus to touch you and make you whole. If you let this happen, you and your community will never be the same. That's what Angie and her kids, the men and women who went to Hooters, and thousands of others who've brought God's party to the streets have discovered.

getting your **feet wet**

Think about people you'd expect to see at the parties you attend. What do they generally have in common?

Now think about the people you rarely or never see at the parties that you attend. Ask yourself, "Why aren't they there?"

Now brainstorm some effective ways you could invite those who aren't like you to Christ's party. Don't stop at just thinking about these ideas; try a few out over the next week.

the **reflection** *pool*

>> Why do you think we have to break some of society's "rules" in order to share Christ's love with our communities?

>> What—if anything—frightens you about the ideas in this reading? How can you get past those fears?

>> What can you change about your own life and your patterns in order to share Christ's love with those who are on the fringes of society?

"WHERE THERE IS
NO VISION,
THE PEOPLE PERISH…"

—PROVERBS 29:18 (KJV)

"Where there is no vision, the
people find another parish."

—Anonymous

READING 20

serving your city through vision

When you read the book of Acts and the letters the apostles sent to the various churches that were spreading like wildfire across the known world, it's pretty clear those churches had more in mind than raising money for building programs or worrying about Sunday school attendance. Their vision was far bigger than that. They pictured entire cities coming into the kingdom of God. And it's a good thing they did because if they had been self-focused, money-minded, or culturally timid, none of us would know Christ today.

When we read Paul's letters to the church in Galatia, the church in Corinth, the church in Philippi, the church in Rome, it's evident that those churches understood God had huge plans for their cities.

Two thousand years later, the vision of many of today's church leaders has shrunk down to surviving financially or maintaining a few ministry programs in a neighborhood or two. Unfortunately, it would be all too easy to write a book called: *Honey, I've Shrunk the Church*! And, while it might get a laugh, it would be heartbreaking to read. Instead of analyzing the systemic faith problems that are shrinking the Church's vision, we'd rather focus on solving them. We'd like every church leader—and for that matter, every follower of Christ—to view the city, town, or metro area in which they live as their own personal parish.

It's time for every Christian to begin connecting with God's heart for the area he or she lives and begin feeling *his* compassion for the people there. Pray that God will open *your* eyes and ears to the people who live in your city— but pray even harder that God will give you his compassion for your city. It's out of this compassion that a true vision will crystallize.

Listen to the compassion of Jesus as he laments over Jerusalem in Matthew 23:37: "O Jerusalem, Jerusalem, the city that kills the prophets and stones God's messengers! How often I have wanted to gather your children together as a hen protects her chicks beneath her wings…" Notice Jesus doesn't gloss over the city's faults, and yet Jesus still hungers to gather its people to himself. Whether you live in Calcutta, Kalamazoo, Cambridge, or any of the thousands of cities and towns that lie in between, Jesus desires the same thing for the people who live there. And the Holy Spirit has a compassionate vision to make that happen in your city. And it's tailor-made to fit your particular culture and situation.

Discovering God's Vision for Your City

One of the best vision clarifying questions is, "What would be happening in my city if Jesus showed up here and all his followers actually started doing everything the Holy Spirit asked of them?"

Don't generalize by saying, "It would be great!" or "Lots of people would be converted." Visualize the *specific* things you and the other Christ-followers in your city would be doing if the Holy Spirit had his way.

When Steve's family first moved to Cincinnati, the grandchildren and great-grandchildren of very quiet, very conservative, and very inhibited German immigrants dominated the city's personality. Many Cincinnatians had been culturally programmed to focus on their families and avoid talking to strangers—especially strangers from California! Fresh from the West

Coast, Steve and Janie experienced a certain cold, standoffishness that helped inspire a powerful vision.

> As our mental picture of what God desired for Cincinnati began to take shape, we got the idea God wanted to use us to help transform our seemingly cold and unfriendly city into a place known for its openness, kindness, and generosity. We began to envision a city full of friendly, openhearted Christ-followers who *loved* reaching out to strangers. In fact, you'd run into them everywhere you went! If you went to the gas station, they'd be offering to wash your windshield or pump your gas for free. If it snowed, they'd show up on your doorstep to shovel your walk. Or you'd find them handing out free hot chocolate to shivering shoppers. And they'd do it all in the name of Jesus with no strings attached!
>
> Over the 20-plus years we've lived here, my wife and I have seen this vision take shape and become more reality than desire. These days, on any given day in Cincinnati, you're likely to find teens, young families, and even those of us over 50 doing acts of kindness in Christ's name. And these people aren't just from our church; they're from scores and even hundreds of other local congregations who've grabbed on to the vision.

Anticipate What God Will Do

Perhaps you've heard it said that, "We tend to reproduce what we anticipate." The way to gain vision is through...*anticipation!* We've seen it over and over again. It really does work this way. Steve was amazed to find that at Kathryn Kuhlman's monthly healing gatherings he attended back in the '70s, more people were healed waiting in line at the Shriner's Auditorium in Los Angeles than during the actual meetings. It was a clear case of *anticipation* and faith in how God's Spirit was about to move in their lives. In fact, anticipation and faith go hand in hand. When you have faith that God can do something, you *anticipate* it. You don't doubt it. You don't think, "Well, maybe...it could happen, I suppose." No—you wait eagerly, *knowing* God's going to do it.

Anticipating his movement. Shivering with excitement because you're about to witness a miracle.

But the thing is, we tend to anticipate results like those we've been "raised in." If you've been in an environment that was dynamic, one where exciting experiences were the norm and where numbers of people came to know Christ on a regular basis—it's likely you have faith that God can do amazing things, and you'll just naturally anticipate and reproduce a spiritual environment just like that. Unfortunately, anticipation can also work against you. If you've come from an environment where the norm is not quite like that—where not much ever happens in the way of spiritual change, where few to none ever come to know Jesus—well, guess what? That's what you'll tend to reproduce. You'll have a barrier of doubt and skepticism to overcome. But nothing is impossible with God. Even if you are someone who grew up without ever experiencing much miraculous change in those around you, God can still create in you a sense of anticipation and faith. God can "biggy-size" your vision!

One of the prime reasons we tend to settle for mediocre spiritual results in our own lives is that we gravitate to the level of vision we feel comfortable with. We seek comfort by nature. Just as some of us are attracted to restaurants that specialize in "comfort foods," we're also drawn to churches that specialize in serving up "comfort spirituality." Maybe this is obvious, but having a vision big enough to encompass your whole city is anything but comfortable. In fact, if you're thinking on a city-wide scale, we can pretty much guarantee you'll feel overwhelmed a great deal of the time. In our experience, real growth and deep spirituality rarely take place inside your comfort zone. Big visions drive us to our knees and compel us to recognize we can't possibly fulfill them on our own. In other words, if God doesn't show up, we're in a heap of trouble. But we *anticipate* and have *faith* that he *will* show up—and in even bigger and more powerful ways than we could think of ourselves.

Take a Risk

You may be distressed by four-letter words, but here's one you need to make friends with: *risk*! Jesus spoke about it frequently and modeled it wherever he went. When he spoke to the woman at the well, and healed sick people on the Sabbath, he was risking his reputation. In Luke 10:1-4, when he sent 72 disciples out to proclaim the kingdom of heaven without any money or bags or even extra sandals, Jesus warned them saying, "I am sending you out as lambs among wolves." In other words, the challenge and the risk were very real—and it's no different for those of us who follow Jesus today.

In Luke 10:17, the 72 returned with joy shouting, "Lord, even the demons obey us when we use your name!" They'd made friends with the risk of hardship and rejection, and they were rewarded with tremendous success. They'd come to *anticipate* that when they stepped out of their comfort zone and beyond their ability to control things—God showed up.

To the non-risk-taker, the specter of catastrophic failure seems huge. It's like stepping out onto an "invisible bridge." It's like the scene from *Indiana Jones and the Last Crusade* where Indiana is reading from his father's handwritten codebook explaining how to go forward. He comes to a huge, seemingly bottomless chasm and the book says to step forward. Indiana thinks it's all a little crazy—until he tosses some dirt onto the invisible bridge and...*bam!* It appears clear as day before him. The impossible was suddenly possible.

In your case and ours, it's experiencing faith that makes the invisible bridge visible. Though the gap between God's vision for your city and what's happening there today may look impossible now, you can trust in your Father and in his vision for your city. As Hebrews 11:1 puts it, "Faith is the confidence that what we hope for will actually happen; it gives us assurance about things we cannot see." The more we step out on the invisible bridge of faith and find out God is dependable and trustworthy, the more confidence we'll have in the reality of his vision for our cities. So go ahead and throw some dirt out there—test it out and see what happens!

Praying for Vision

One way to get a vision for your city is to walk around its various neighborhoods and pray. To experience the heart of God for the city in which you live, it's necessary to do some significant walking around. Though you can cover lots of geography in a very short time by driving, walking and praying allows you to slow down and catch a much better sense of what the Spirit is saying about your town. In our travels we've noticed that God seems to speak *different* things about different parts of any given town. As odd as it may sound, by just walking a few blocks from one part of town to another the spiritual "atmosphere" can change dramatically.

One place where we've had tremendous success is in Cincinnati's Tri-County Mall. There are nearly always families with children out for some leisurely shopping, retired folks out for a stroll, and teenagers hanging out with friends. Spiritually speaking, it has also turned out to be a very open place for outreach. It's nearly perfect for all kinds of practical acts of service like wrapping shoppers' holiday presents for free or providing "umbrella service" from the parking lot to the main entrance on rainy days.

But less than half a mile away, there's an area packed with poor families living in government-subsidized housing. Police have found methamphetamine labs there and fatal shootings are commonplace. It's actually a fairly nice-looking neighborhood on the outside, but spiritually it's an extremely oppressive environment. So in gaining a vision for reaching the people of our city, we've had to think differently about reaching residents of this neighborhood. We have to break through levels of fear and mistrust that are far more intense—but God is not about to abandon this neighborhood. He's just called us to reach out to it in different ways. Things like offering free bread and bags of groceries have opened many doors and hearts to Jesus in this community.

Within another half a mile there's a different community called Glendale. Glendale is one of the most affluent areas per square foot in Cincinnati. Many homes there are large mansions built in the 1800s by wealthy industrialists and their families. The people living in them now have completely different spiritual needs from those in the neighborhood just down the street. Their wealth and social positions have left many of them feeling empty, hungry for authentic friends, or exhausted from a stressful life in corporate America. In many ways, wealth and social position can be even more spiritually oppressive than poverty—and we had to notice that before we could begin reaching that area of town with Jesus' love. That's right, our vision for reaching our city had to include them, too. God had not abandoned them any more than he had abandoned the neighborhood down the street. We organized business and family-oriented outreaches and short-term mission trips to places like Mexico City. These efforts proved life changing for many of the people in Glendale. Though few of them would have considered themselves as "needy," getting them involved in helping others often opened a door to their own spiritual poverty.

Obviously, the kind of neighborhood-by-neighborhood vision we're talking about doesn't spring into existence fully formed in a day or even a month. It grows as the Christ-followers of your town begin to take spiritual ownership and responsibility for what's happening in your city.

It's Not About *Your* Church, It's About *The* Church

There will be people who are wonderfully effective serving a particular neighborhood or population. So it's tempting to just let them go and "do their thing" and let them compete with each other for the money and resources to get the job done. But that's not the picture the New Testament gives us for reaching our cities and towns for Christ.

When the Apostle Paul wrote to the Christians who were working to reach the largest city in the known world, here is what he said:

"Just as each of us has one body with many members, and these members do not all have the same function, so in Christ we who are many form one body, and each member belongs to all the others. We have different gifts, according to the grace given us" (ROMANS 12:4-6a, NIV).

This Scripture speaks of different "gifts" and special "grace" being given to everyone who serves. This means *you*. You're an indispensable part of the body of Christ. You have unique, irreplaceable work to do in accomplishing Christ's vision. The Holy Spirit can help you discover the specific gifts God wants to pour through you. If you don't know what your gifts are yet—or how you can use your gifts—start serving over and over in different places until you discover what you love and experience the power of God overflowing from you and your life. As you serve and God flows through you, you'll begin to anticipate the good things God will do through you.

But that's not all. Instead of just doing *your* thing, you've got to work closely with the other parts of the body to accomplish "God's thing" in your city and in the world. The parts of the body don't work when they're separated or disconnected. The only way that you can do the huge things it takes to impact an entire city with Christ's love, is by linking arms with lots of other individuals and churches. It's ridiculous to imagine for a moment that any one person, group, church, or denomination is going to accomplish the Great Commission on its own. We need God *and* one another if we hope to reach our cultures. That's God's vision for pouring his love out in your city and helping you overflow with his living water into the world.

getting your **feet wet**

Think of the needs of people who live near you in your city or town. If you live in a rural area think about the special needs of people who live in your county.

Get a map and look at the various neighborhoods that surround yours. If you don't have a map, you can go online to www.earth.google.com and download free software that will allow you to type in your address and look down on your house from outer space.

Using your home as a center point, look to see the other neighborhoods within a mile, five miles, and 15 miles of your house. Now pick an area and pray for what you know are the needs of the people who live there, and for the churches and ministries who are already sharing Christ's love in those places. If you don't know enough about the needs of those areas, go there this week and find out.

the **reflection** *pool*

>> What is it about your city that you love? What makes your city special? How could those special aspects of your city translate into God's vision for your city?

>> What would be happening in your city if Jesus showed up there and all his followers actually started doing everything the Holy Spirit asked of them?

>> What's one way you can personally become a part of God's vision for your city?

the deep end

WATER GIVE-AWAY

In order to take God to your community and to people you wouldn't normally hang around...well...you have to get out there and be *with* your community and the people who live there.

Use this Deep End experience to serve your community as you spend time with the people who live there.

By yourself or with your small group, plan an afternoon to spend time in a part of your city *you don't normally visit.* Take coolers full of bottled water with you and give them away to the people you meet. (If it's colder outside, consider giving away hot chocolate.)

As you give away the water, look for opportunities to talk with people. Ask questions about the community, places to work, schools, churches, and so on. These questions can open up doors to further conversations. But be considerate: If people are in a hurry or don't appear interested in chatting, don't push; offer those people a bottle of water and a smile before they move on. Also remember not to push people to talk about spiritual matters. Let the conversations flow naturally and just share God's love through your actions. Of course, if someone asks why you're giving away water, you can always say: "We're just trying to show God's love in a practical way!"

group
discussion questions

*Use these questions during your small-group time and dia-
logue together about the fourth week of* Outflow *readings.*

>> What comes to mind when you think of ways you
can personally overflow Jesus' love into your community?

>> Reading 17 challenges Christians to listen to their
communities. Where can you go to listen to people
in your community? Once there, how will you listen
to the people around you?

>> What places in your community do you already go
to on a regular basis? How can you connect with the
people in those places?

>> Reading 19 talks about serving *everyone*—even those
who frighten us or make us uncomfortable. What
can you change about your own life and your patterns in order to share Christ's love with those who
are on the fringes of society?

>> Reading 20 discusses God's "vision" for cities.
What is it about your city that you love? What makes
your city special? How could those special aspects
of your city translate into God's vision for your city?

OUTFLOW

you

your family
& friends

your
community

your
world

outward toward your world

"IMITATE GOD, THEREFORE, IN EVERYTHING
YOU DO, BECAUSE YOU ARE HIS DEAR CHILDREN.
LIVE A LIFE FILLED WITH LOVE, FOLLOWING
THE EXAMPLE OF CHRIST. HE LOVED US AND
OFFERED HIMSELF AS A SACRIFICE FOR US,
A PLEASING AROMA TO GOD."

—EPHESIANS 5:1-2

"It could be that one of the greatest hindrances to
evangelism is the poverty of our own experience."

—Billy Graham

READING 21

the ends of the earth

As you catch God's vision for bringing the good news of Jesus to the world, it's common to assume the way to begin is to try to do "something really big for God!" That's certainly "the American way," but in our experience, bigger isn't usually better. We recommend doing something profound: *Start small.* Remember our motto: *small things* done with great love will change the world. Small seeds grow into tall trees, and they're small for a reason—to take greatest advantage of the tiniest of openings and opportunities.

Jesus could've chosen huge celebrities from the religious or political world to spread his gospel. It would have made sense to use their automatic name recognition and network of friends in high places to "build buzz" and gain "crowd appeal." But Jesus chose little-known people from the least-known provinces and villages as his anointed messengers. The "dream team" he handpicked for the job was made up of former fishermen, a reformed tax collector, a rehabilitated prostitute or two, and others even more obscure. We think he might have chosen them for the same reason God picked a stuttering sheepherder, named Moses, to free his chosen people from slavery. And why God chose the youngest son of a shepherd to become the greatest king of Israel. God can work through anyone and everyone. If you've ever felt too small, or unskilled, or unworthy to be a world-changer, God has remarkable news for you—you are chosen!

Hard to believe, but it's true nonetheless. God wants to pour his love into you and through you in world-changing ways. Jesus said, "God authorized and commanded me to commission you: Go out and train everyone you meet, far and near, in this way of life, marking them by baptism in the threefold name: Father, Son, and Holy Spirit. Then instruct them in the practice of all I have commanded you" (Matthew 28:18-20a, *The Message*). Jesus was talking to you—and to all of us who know we don't have what it takes to pull this off. That's why the very next thing he says is, "I'll be with you as you do this, day after day after day, right up to the end of the age" (MATTHEW 28:20b, *The Message*). You may *feel* unimportant, but with Jesus always at your side, nothing can stop you!

"Making disciples of all nations" naturally flows out from a vibrant relationship with God—the source of all love. As you listen to God, love God, and share your heart with God, it's only natural to want to serve others in God's name. Your desire and capacity for serving the Lord may start out small, but it will increase. The more you serve, the more you'll experience God, and the greater your love for him will naturally become. This is how your spirit is meant to grow. The Bible points out that the more you mature spiritually, the more you'll "reflect the Lord's glory" as you "are being transformed into his likeness with ever-increasing glory, which comes from the Lord, who is the Spirit" (2 CORINTHIANS 3:18, NIV).

It's Not Big Business

Contrary to what you may have been led to believe by television and the movies, changing the world is a pretty simple and humble process. Though it's serious business, it's often really fun, too. You don't have to write best-selling books or become a missionary in some remote South American tribe. World-changing opportunities will present themselves when you step out your door. One group of Christ-followers we know had a simple idea as they watched people walking down the boardwalk at the beach in Santa Cruz, California. They'd noticed lots of people uncomfortably brushing sand off their feet as they walked along and wondered, "Didn't Jesus teach his followers to serve by washing feet?" Shannon, one of the group members, tells the story:

> Our church friends said, "No one is going to let you touch their feet! You guys are crazy!" But they couldn't have been more wrong.
>
> We set up at the Beach Boardwalk in Santa Cruz about 1:00 in the afternoon. There were just a handful of us. We chose a spot right at the entrance to the beach. Our supplies consisted of two fold-up chairs, two plastic containers, paper towels, liquid Dial soap, a five-gallon jug to haul water, and a heart for the lost.

Our opening line went something like, "Hi. Would you like to sit down and let us rinse the sand off of your feet?"

We had very few refusals! In fact, we were so busy that we actually had people lined up! We took about three minutes with each person. We silently prayed as we worked, but when asked, about 95 percent of the people let us pray out loud with them.

There were many heart-touching encounters that day, but there is one I'll always remember. One gentleman from Asia kept calling one of our team members "Jesus." When we tried to correct him and explain who Jesus was, he replied, "I know who Jesus is, *and you are just like him.*"

We all knew that if we showed up and were faithful, Jesus would show up, too. And let me tell you, seeing people on that beach through Jesus' eyes was absolutely amazing!

Maybe this story doesn't sound particularly earth shattering, but we think it's exactly how God likes us to go about changing the world. The little group of boardwalk foot-washers was responding in the spirit of Jesus to a simple need they observed. In fact, what they did calls to mind Ephesians 5:1-2 which tells us to, "Imitate God, therefore, in everything you do, because you are his dear children. Live a life filled with love, following the example of Christ. He loved us and offered himself as a sacrifice for us, a pleasing aroma to God."

When we think of Jesus giving himself up as a sacrifice to God, we're likely to focus exclusively on one *event* that took place on the cross and forget the *lifetime* of service that preceded it. Jesus was "giving himself up" all the time. From the moment he woke up in the morning, to the time he went to sleep every night, his was a *lifestyle* dedicated to serving the Father.

It isn't one big moment in your life—one big act of service—that will change the world. It's the little things. The everyday things. It's the way you live your life moment-to-moment, day-to-day...*today*. Imitate Jesus in how you connect with *each* person you meet and, like Jesus, you'll begin impacting one life at a time as you go about your daily routine. Look, listen, and open your heart to the opportunities presented to you *each day* and you won't just read about miraculous events in the Bible, you'll actually play a part in them.

It's what happened to Dave in the wake of Hurricane Katrina.

"My wife, Pam, is a real dog lover, so when we went south to help survivors of the Gulf Coast hurricanes, she was worried about all the pets stranded by the storms. So before we could head home, she insisted that we spend an afternoon volunteering at a Humane Society that was reuniting storm victims with their rescued dogs. I grumbled that God had called us to help people—not puppy dogs—but like an obedient husband went along anyway...and ended up being glad I did.

When we got there, Pam went to work on the phones and I went to work with several other men loading huge trailers with hundreds of 20-pound and 50-pound bags of donated dog food. It was hot, sweaty work and the trailers kept coming. When we stopped for a break, I caught my breath and struck up a conversation with Ron, a guy I'd been working with. When Ron asked me how I'd come to be loading dog food, I explained, "My wife and I believe God sent us from Cincinnati to the Gulf Coast to listen to people caught up in the storms and help them out however we could. So here we are!"

Ron shook his head in apparent disbelief and said, "God must really be out to get me!" When I asked what he meant, Ron told me the following story:

"I had a little farm just outside of New Orleans until everything I owned got washed away in the storm surge. Somehow I survived until the soldiers came and evacuated me to the Astrodome. I just sat on my cot staring at the ceiling and thinking: *Oh God, I don't think I can stand another day in this place with nothing to do.* Then a lady and her husband walked up to me.

They didn't know me from Adam, but said they thought God wanted them to invite me to live in their house until I got back on my feet. I was kind of suspicious at first—I even asked to see their driver's licenses, but they turned out to be the *real deal*. They helped me locate my son who I hadn't heard from since the storm and I moved in with them a couple of days ago. Now here you are saying God sent you from Cincinnati to listen to me. I can't help but think he's trying to get my attention.

Back home in New Orleans, I've worked with the Humane Society for the last 30 years. So I thought the least I could do to show my gratitude for being alive was to come down here and volunteer to help others in the best way I know how."

As Ron and I went back to work heaving more sacks of dog food on the trailers, Ron couldn't stop talking about how grateful he was for what God was doing in his situation.

"I've heard *preaching* all my life," he said. "But until now, I never really believed God had much interest in me *personally.* If being here is what it took to show me, I'm OK with that."

Ron wasn't 100 percent ready to ask Christ into his life on the spot, but he was asking tons of important questions. He was knocking, seeking, and asking...and God was answering by sending him folks who were willing to do whatever it took to meet Ron where he was. God's love was overflowing into Ron's world from complete strangers. And it left Ron hungry and thirsty for more. In our experience, that's one of God's favorite ways to change the world. It's not up to you or any of us to make it happen, *it's already happening.* God just wants us to join in.

Pay Attention!

If you pay attention, God will reveal lots of simple ways to reach out to the world. Here's one last story for this reading...

Chris and a group from his congregation were visiting a church called Nuevo Pacto in Monterrey, Mexico. Church members wanted to reach out into their community, and together with their visitors they came up with the plan of giving away free tacos and soft drinks. So they set up their taco table near the church on an access road that runs parallel to a main road in Monterrey. Chris tells what happened:

> We made signs from old bed sheets that read, *"¡Hoy taco y sodas Gratis! ¡Muy divertido!"* (Free tacos and sodas today! Lots of fun!)
>
> We served up about 1,200 tacos to the 250 to 275 people who showed up, telling each one, "Christo te Ama" (Christ loves you.)
>
> Two people prayed to receive Christ on the spot! Many others picked up small fliers about the Nuevo Pacto church along with their tacos. Afterward, one man from the neighborhood kept walking around the church until the pastor invited him in. As Pastor Renee was talking with him, the man saw a sign announcing a "buy a chair program" for church members (they were renting chairs from a local company at the time). The man smiled and said, "Here are 200 pesos for a chair...I will be here to fill it this weekend. See you Sunday."

No matter what city or country you're in, reaching out with lots of everyday acts of kindness and connecting people with the compassionate heart of Jesus is a really fun way to change the world. You can be part of it if you're willing to "put your ears on" and listen for the openings God provides. We'll talk about that some more in the next few readings.

getting your **feet wet**

Talk to God and ask him to point out some small need you might help to meet or a simple way you could add a little cheer to someone's day. When something simple and doable comes to mind, don't hesitate. Set the wheels of kindness in motion.

If nothing comes to mind, ask a friend to join you in coming up with some small act of kindness you can do together. Again, don't wait…just go and give it a try.

the **reflection** *pool*

>> Which story in this reading gave you a more positive—and achievable—outlook on reaching the world with God's love?

>> Why do you think it's important for each Christian—individually—to take a personal interest in changing the world for God?

>> How could you—or your church or small group—personally join in with what God's already doing to reach the world with his love?

"AND HE SAID: 'I TELL
YOU THE TRUTH, UNLESS
YOU CHANGE AND BECOME
LIKE LITTLE CHILDREN,
YOU WILL NEVER ENTER THE
KINGDOM OF HEAVEN.' "

—MATTHEW 18:3 (NIV)

"God loves us the way we
are, but he loves us too much
to leave us that way."

—Leighton Ford

READING 22

listening for a change

Steve will never forget how Rose introduced herself on the Sunday morning they met. "Hi, I'm Rose," she said quietly, "…and I'm dying."

Now that she had his attention, Rose went on to explain that she had a serious blood disease that the doctors could do nothing about. She'd been through all kinds of treatments, but now they were giving her three months to live. With a look of forlorn resignation in her eyes, Rose said she'd live just long enough to celebrate her 70th birthday and "that would be that."

Though he's not in the habit of responding this way to folks with terminal illnesses, Steve felt the Spirit prompting him to speak up in a somewhat audacious way.

" Well Rose, I'm sorry to hear that you're dying, but wouldn't you rather go out with a bang instead of a whimper?" I said.

Not surprisingly, Rose did a big double take and with a shocked expression demanded, "What did you just say?"

I repeated myself and continued, "This week a bunch of us are going to deliver about 100 bags of groceries and lots of clothes to single parents in a poor part of town. When we give them the food and clothes, we'll offer to pray for them. Don't you think going with us might be a great first step toward going out with a bang?" After a moment of hesitation, Rose agreed to come with us.

A few days later we went out to deliver our bags of food and groceries. Rose was quiet and a little reserved. Mostly she watched and helped carry bags while other volunteers knocked on doors and prayed for people. At the end of our deliveries, she remarked to me, "You know, I think I can do this. It looks fun actually. I think I'll come back next week."

Indeed Rose did come back the following week, and the week after that. And it was on that third week when something powerful happened to our dear Rose. I was blessed enough to be with her when it happened.

I was carrying the groceries. Though she was shy and retiring by nature, Rose had now gained enough confidence to engage the strangers we were serving in conversation. At one of our stops, we were invited into a family's apartment and introduced to "Grandma," a woman who was younger than Rose, but suffering from diabetes. Grandma's legs were very swollen, and she hadn't been out of her wheelchair in over 18 months. She needed major assistance from at least two adults just to go to the bathroom.

When Rose asked if there was anything we could pray for, Grandma spoke up saying, "I just want to be able to wiggle my ankles. I haven't been able to move them in almost two years. I'm worried I'm going to lose my legs to this disease."

Rose whispered in my ear, "Oh my, this is over my head." But I encouraged her just to pray a simple prayer and let God take it from there.

Though Rose looked at me with a pleading look, I said, "I'm sorry, I'm fresh out of prayers this morning—it's up to you. Why don't you just say something like, 'God make these ankles move, in Jesus' name!' "

Rose said, "That sounds silly." But she prayed it anyway.

One minute passed, and Grandma said, "I feel some tingling in my ankles." Rose was surprised but pleased, so she asked if she could pray a little more. This time the tingling increased. So Rose prayed a third time with real gusto. This time Grandma not only wiggled her ankles, she was able to move them about 4 inches up and down! To Rose and me it didn't seem like much, but you should have seen her family react. It was as if the Publishers Clearing House had shown up at their door with an oversized check for a million dollars.

Rose's life changed in that moment. She not only became a more devoted participant in our church's outreach, she began praying for people regularly, and started giving out clothing and food two extra days a week.

Months passed, then years, then a couple of decades (that's right, I said decades), and Rose is still going strong. Recently I asked her about her "fatal" disease. She laughed and told me, "Now all of those doctors are dead and here I am, still plugging away, fit as a fiddle!"

Rose's friends from church recently helped her celebrate her 90th birthday. It was a huge party (something like the ending of the movie It's a Wonderful Life, but on steroids). Over 700 people showed up.

Everyone knows that I am very close to Rose so they asked me to say a few words at the party. So I cuddled up to where she sat in a high-back chair. As I began to speak, I broke down sobbing. I couldn't control myself for a few minutes. Spontaneously the crowd of hundreds all began to weep—all of us for the same reason.

When I pulled myself together, I finally said, "I'm only 50 now, but when I grow up, I want to be just like Rose!" Everybody cheered because they knew she lives every day for Jesus and others, not for herself. She has borne incredible fruit in countless lives while defying a medical death sentence in her own. The power of Jesus has been living in her and pouring out through her. Rose's willingness to trust God and begin stepping out in faith are what God's kingdom is all about.

Rose's story is a great example of how much more fruitfulness God can bring into our lives if we're willing to listen to God and do what he says. We're certainly not promising an extra 20 years of life to every terminally ill person reading this book. We're simply making the point that, in Rose's case at least, there's been something incredibly healing about getting her mind off her own problems and focusing instead on letting God's love overflow through her into the lives of others.

Ralph Waldo Emerson wisely said, "People wish to be settled; only as far as they are unsettled is there any hope for them." Rose chose to listen to Steve's unsettling invitation to make the days she had left count for God. It would have been much easier to ignore him or even to take offense. But as Hebrews 10:24 puts it, she allowed God to use what Steve said to "spur [her] on toward love and good deeds" (NIV). The Holy Spirit's urging can be a gentle nudge or a sharp spur in the ribs. Either way, it's designed to get your attention off of yourself and the countless things that distract you, and onto God's purposes.

New Frontiers

Everyday of your life, if you pay attention, the Holy Spirit is urging you toward a deeper and richer experience with God. If you let him, God will guide you beyond your comfort zone into new frontiers of personal healing and change. Contrary to a lot of the teaching that's out there though, the change you're looking for probably won't come from meditating on what's going on in your own heart. And it certainly won't come from focusing on your personal problems or limitations. In most cases, the path to growth begins with focusing outward on how God is calling you to bless others.

Unfortunately most of us prefer established routine to the adventure of growth. We're so prone to avoiding the discomfort associated with it that Hebrews has to remind us "The Holy Spirit says, 'Today when you hear his voice, don't harden your hearts...' " (HEBREWS 3:7-8a).

You say you want a dynamic, living relationship with God? The Spirit says open your ears and your eyes, and soften your heart. Let God's compassion for the world and all the people around you make you uncomfortable. And start seeking God for small things you can do with great love. Like Rose, you may find yourself saying, "You know, I think I can do this." And what seemed scary will actually become more fun than you ever imagined.

> You'll be amazed at what kinds of things will touch people's hearts. A young couple named John and Carol Christian from a village near Madras, India telephoned Steve long-distance to get some guidance about ways to reach out in their community. The phone connection wasn't very good, but Steve still had a great time explaining some of his favorite outreach ideas to them. A few weeks later, John called back on a line with a much clearer connection. He said, "I love your idea about the free cow wash! We tried it and people here really loved it."
>
> When Steve finished laughing, he clarified, "I didn't say 'free cow wash'...I said 'free car wash!'"
>
> This time it was John doing the laughing. Then he explained, "Well that's OK, a cow wash is much better here, because we have more cows than cars!"
>
> As John and Carol have continued reaching out, they've come up with more ideas that sounded just as crazy to Steve. Having grown up in Kansas, Steve remembers being forced to drink buttermilk and hating it. But John and Carol found that distributing cold, spiced buttermilk was the perfect thing to help workers beat the heat in India. They focused on bringing this traditional refreshment to traffic policemen and construction workers in downtown Madras. They raised over 26,000 rupees (about $500) from members of their congregation to buy supplies to distribute the buttermilk and it turned out to be worth every rupee. Who would have guessed—buttermilk was a big hit!

There are so many fun, creative ways to communicate God's love and help you grow closer to God in the process. And it's up to you to put them into practice.

James 1:5 says, "If any of you lacks wisdom, he should ask God, who gives generously to all without finding fault, and it will be given to him" (NIV). So if you don't know where to start, don't feel bad. God is willing to pour out the ideas and the resources you need to carry them out. Begin by inviting the Holy Spirit to give you a fresh, creative perspective. Then listen up! Often, the perspective you're looking for will come through an unexpected conversation as it did for Rose, and John and Carol in the stories we told earlier. Or sometimes it will come to you in the form of a verse of Scripture or a simple word-picture that pops into your mind. God communicates with his followers in all sorts of ways—just listen carefully for his voice!

There's More...

God wants you to reach out and love people, but it isn't just to help them or to change the world. It's also one of God's favorite ways of enriching your life, healing your brokenness, and making you a little more like Jesus. First John 4:16-17 promises, "And so we know and rely on the love God has for us. God is love. Whoever lives in love lives in God, and God in him. In this way, love is made complete among us so that we will have confidence on the day of judgment, because in this world we are like him" (NIV).

It's hard to imagine the world-changing richness of the life God has in mind for you and the people you serve, but it sure sounds good. To embrace it you'll have to significantly expand your capacity to love. That's what we'll talk about next.

getting your feet wet

Think of a needy person or a growth opportunity that causes you to feel a little uncomfortable.

What about that person or situation triggers the uncomfortable feeling?

How do you think God might be able to help you turn your discomfort into something positive?

....

....

....

Now put it into action! Pray and ask God what you can do in this situation today.

the
reflection
pool

>> Are you settled or unsettled? Why? How might becoming "unsettled" help you reach out to the world with God's love?

>> When has focusing outward helped you grow personally? Describe the situation.

>> How can you listen for the ways God wants you to reach out to the world with his love?

"MAKE EVERY EFFORT TO
ADD TO YOUR FAITH
GOODNESS; AND TO
GOODNESS, KNOWLEDGE; AND
TO KNOWLEDGE,
SELF-CONTROL; AND
TO SELF-CONTROL,
PERSEVERANCE; AND TO
PERSEVERANCE, GODLINESS;
AND TO GODLINESS,
BROTHERLY KINDNESS;
AND TO BROTHERLY
KINDNESS, LOVE."

—2 PETER 1:5-7 (NIV)

"Loving the world at
large can only be done
by loving face-to-face
the world that is
not so distant."

—Calvin Miller

READING 23

love in action

Without a doubt, John 3:16 is the most quoted verse of the New Testament. You've probably heard it quoted hundreds of times at church or on television or in conversations with followers of Christ. It goes, "For God so loved the world, that he gave his only begotten Son, that whosoever believeth in him should not perish, but have everlasting life" (KJV).

OK, God loves the world and Jesus died to bring eternal life to anyone who believes in him. What does that have to do with you? If you believe, there is a wonderful promise here for you. You won't perish and you'll have eternal life. But that's not all—if it's true that we love because God first loved us (1 JOHN

4:19), and if it's true that Jesus calls us to love each other in the same way he loved us (JOHN 15:12)—then this verse (JOHN 3:16) is more than just a promise to us...it's also a call to action for every Christ-follower. God so *loved* the world...that he did something about it! God's love is a love of action, of sacrifice, of immense generosity. And it's how our love should be, too. God *so loved* the world—let it be true that every single Christian so *loves* the world.

A while back, about 55 believers from a church in Florida teamed up to show the generous love we're talking about to the community of Pensacola. They used all sorts of practical ways to communicate God's kindness to the people there. They washed cars for free, gave away free hamburgers, hot dogs, and cold drinks, and went door-to-door handing out free light bulbs. Others brought bathroom-cleaning supplies from home and scrubbed about 40 restrooms in local shops and gas stations explaining to all who asked, "We're just looking for small ways to serve people that say 'God loves you!'" John, the pastor who was leading this outreach tells a story of one of the encounters they had that day...

> After the bathroom team finished, I took them to get a cold drink at a local gas station. Tina, one of the cleaners, told us someone had snuck a twenty-dollar bill into her cleaning bucket and she was wondering what to do with it.
>
> I suggested that we stick around the gas station and add five dollars of "free" gas to the tanks of the next four people that came in. The first customer who came in was a little boy. His dad had given him a small plastic bowl filled with pennies to prepay for what little fuel it would buy. Talk about divine appointments! This was one for sure. When Tina gave him the extra money, the little boy's eyes practically popped out of his head and neither he nor his father could believe what was happening.

The little boy, his father, and several hundred other Floridians got a little taste of God's generous love that day, but that's not all that happened. The 55 Christians carrying out kind actions in God's name got a tiny taste of what it means to *so love the world* like God does. They reached out beyond the walls of their church and experienced what 2 Peter 1:4 is talking about when it says we can "share [God's] divine nature." They felt and smelled and tasted a bit of what it's like to give themselves for others. They saw the surprised looks on people's faces and they witnessed in many people a hunger to believe in a truly generous God.

In the same letter in which Pastor John told us the stories above, he also mentioned that another young man they'd served decided to trust Jesus was baptized the very next Sunday. After his congregation witnessed this baptism and heard the young man's story, other church members started talking about how they too might go out and start serving the world in Christ's name. They had seen the results of God's love in action—and were getting excited, thinking that perhaps, just possibly, they could participate in it, too. Witnessing Christ's sacrificial generosity at just about any level is contagious. It will motivate you and the people around you to action far more than guilt or duty ever could. And it helps overcome dangerous and negative *imprinting*.

Overcoming the Negative Imprints

Perhaps you've heard of how newly hatched ducklings and goslings connect with the first moving object they see. Maybe you've watched those humorous videos or seen the silly pictures of baby ducks trooping along after a dog or a cat—thinking they were following their mother. Scientists once thought this bond was imprinted irreversibly on the bird's nervous system, but fortunately for the ducks and for us, that's not always the case. This is important because it turns out that imprinting isn't just a duck-thing, it's a spiritual-thing, too. Many of us who set out to follow Christ often end up mirroring the behavior of the human leaders we knew in the early stages of our spiritual growth; for better or worse, we are imprinted with the outlooks, values, and behavior of those leaders.

Because of negative spiritual imprinting, many of us who set out to follow the generous ways of Jesus, often end up living in stingy ways more akin to the Pharisees of Jesus' day. Instead of *loving the world* in ways consistent with the love God modeled in John 3:16—instead of reaching out with practical acts of generosity—we allow ourselves to become imprinted with some rather opposite ideals. We become sour, judgmental, and argumentative. We follow the role models who have imprinted their values on us—role models who are found in far too many religious organizations and churches today.

Too often, we eagerly parade after these role models, until we too are displaying similar attributes—selfishness, subtle hatred, fear of those who are different, the list goes on...This doesn't mean we won't frequently speak of God's love, but what we follow is often more foreign to Christ's compassion than a dog is to a duck!

In Matthew 23:13 Jesus proclaims, "Woe to you teachers of the law and Pharisees, you hypocrites! You shut the kingdom of heaven in men's faces. You yourselves do not enter, nor will you let those enter who are trying to" (NIV). Jesus pronounced this false, mean, and miserly spirituality as antithetical to his kingdom of love. One of the top reasons we believe the watching world doesn't respect the church in America and Western Europe is that, more often than not, we've fallen into the trap of disconnecting Jesus' message from the caring and sacrificial actions crucial to validating its authenticity.

Steve makes a practice of conversing with his restaurant servers about their life stories...and about their favorite and least favorite days to work. Almost without exception, they say the same thing regarding their least favorite day to wait on tables: "I hate coming in on Sundays," they say, "especially right after church lets out." They'll frequently go on to say that church people are often the rudest, most demanding, and least generous people who come in each week. If they leave a tip at all, it's 10 percent or less. It may be that all the servers Steve talks to are just prejudiced, but it's more likely they're honestly relating a depressing truth we'd rather not hear.

Getting Out

We hate to talk about discouraging problems without pointing you toward solutions that you can put into practice. So, beyond being more friendly and generous to waiters and waitresses, how can you overcome the negative spiritual imprinting to which you've been exposed? A good way to challenge the less-than-loving spiritual behaviors you've become comfortable with is to get out and spend time around people who don't believe or behave as you do. We know this may go against what you've been taught, but we think we're on solid biblical ground here. We've looked at it before, but let's look at Jesus' last command again:

"Jesus came and told his disciples, "I have been given all authority in heaven and on earth. Therefore, go and make disciples of all the nations, baptizing them in the name of the Father and the Son and the Holy Spirit. Teach these new disciples to obey all the commands I have given you. And be sure of this: I am with you always, even to the end of the age" (MATTHEW 28:19-20).

Maybe this seems a little obvious, but how is it possible to *go and make disciples* without getting around people who *aren't yet disciples*?

Maybe you've been imprinted with the false notion that evangelistic outreach is for experts, but you won't find such a notion coming from Jesus. And as we've said before, most people who come to Jesus don't come because of experts. They come because a caring friend walked the road to faith with them.

OK, here comes another obvious idea. It's not possible for you to help a friend become a disciple unless you have a friend or three *who aren't disciples yet*. We're not trying to make you feel guilty if you don't have any friends who aren't Christians. We just want to encourage you to step out and be a little friendlier and more generous to those outside your familiar circle of friends.

One way to do this is to get around naturally generous and friendly people and learn from them. This may sound like heresy to some, but one way to go into all the world is to volunteer somewhere *outside of your church* like the Humane Society, Habitat for Humanity, or the National Kidney Foundation. Organizations like these do noble things and are constantly on the lookout for warm bodies to help. They're also great places to rub shoulders and make friends with people who want to make a difference. It's amazing how open these compassionate people can be to an authentic relationship with Jesus.

Another idea is to go take an art class or another of the educational offerings at your local YMCA or Chamber of Commerce. It's a great way to build relationships with the people who come every week. Or kill two birds with one stone by joining a sports team: You can exercise physically *and* reach out to teammates spiritually at the same time.

If you've been living a form of Christianity that's predominantly inward-focused, it will take some effort to change your mind-set. Just remember God loves the world so much he sent his Son. God wants to send you, too. If you're willing to represent him, you can be God's hands and feet and voice in the culture around you. God doesn't want you to be content just donating money to outreach experts who are more comfortable doing it than you are. God wants you to go out to the spiritually hungry and thirsty, because that's where he went when he was on earth (MATTHEW 9:9-12). We're not trying to fan your sense of guilt or duty. We just want you to get "hooked" on loving like Jesus. Here's the kind of love were talking about:

Jesus' love is active, not passive; it doesn't wait for people to show up at church. It's like the father in the story of the prodigal son in Luke 15. While the wayward son "was still a long way off, his father saw him and was filled with compassion for him; he ran to his son, threw his arms around him and kissed him" (NIV). Isn't that the kind of energy we need to *imprint* on our lives and the lives of every Christ-follower? God's love is directed outward, not just inward. Luke 19:10 tells us that, "For the Son of Man came to seek and to save those who are lost." Jesus couldn't stay in heaven where he was comfortable because Jesus knew his Father's passion for gathering those he loves under his wings.

If we embrace Jesus' love for the world, we'll start acting like him—not one day, way down the road, but *today*. We'll start living differently, and with the help of God's Spirit working inside us, we'll begin treating those he loves differently, too. We won't do it perfectly, but we'll do it persistently over and over and over…until we begin to think and feel and become more like Jesus. That's the goal of our faith and the hope of the gospel—to fully experience the love of John 3:16, you have to partake of it yourself *and* share it with others. God loves you so much that he won't be content until you are so full of his goodness, compassion, honesty, and kindness that it will overflow into the lives all around you and even to the uttermost parts of the earth. The next reading will talk about how to live the love you've been given and share it far beyond the borders of your life.

getting your **feet wet**

Get five 3x5 cards or sticky notes and copy John 3:16 on each one—in your own handwriting. Strategically tape the cards on your bathroom mirror, on the back of your front door, on the dashboard of your car, on your telephone at work, and on your checkbook cover or wallet.

Whenever you see one of these cards during the next week, ask God, "How can I so love the world today?" Pray that God would place someone or some-place specifically on your mind. When he does, think of some little thing you can do for that person or the people in that place—something that says, "God loves you." Then go do it. When you're done write what you did on one of your five cards.

Once you've written on all five of your cards, take a few minutes to reflect and thank God for the ways he's making the love of John 3:16 a living and growing part of who you are.

the **reflection** *pool*

>> How might *so loving the world* change the way you see the people around you?

>> Where can you go, or what can you do, to naturally engage with more people who are not yet disciples of Christ?

>> How could loving the world become a part of your lifestyle and not just something you make yourself do?

"GREATER IS HE THAT IS
IN YOU, THAN HE THAT IS
IN THE WORLD."

—1 JOHN 4:4

"The world is what I
share with others."

—Martin Heidegger

READING 24

sharing with everyone!

Fear. It's the number one reason followers of Christ give for their reluctance to talk to others about Jesus. It's not so much that we fear that people will reject Christ; we're mostly just scared stiff that they'll pigeonhole *us*. We're not stupid; we've seen those who are vocal about their Christianity ridiculed behind their backs. And we know being branded as a "fundamentalist" or a "Jesus freak" means being looked down upon. "No thanks!" we say, "That's not for me!"

If it's how you feel, we can't blame you. The way a lot of people attempt to "share their faith" is rude, condescending, and socially insensitive. Even as fellow followers of Christ, we can't stand being around folks who hammer others with unsolicited religious monologues. We love them and know they mean well, but the heavy-handed evangelistic methods some people employ make it harder for the rest of us to share the love of Jesus.

> Larry, a business owner with a strong personal faith in Jesus, had a religiously obnoxious employee named Stan. Though other employees shunned and mocked him, Stan was very proud of the fact that he could make a four-point gospel presentation to a full elevator in the time it took for the doors to close on one floor and open on the next.
>
> Larry had to call Stan into his office to talk to Stan about the angry complaints he was getting from nearly everyone else in the company. Exasperated, Larry tried to reason with him saying,
>
> "You aren't converting anybody, Stan. You're turning them against Jesus."
>
> In a disturbingly vindictive tone, Stan explained, "I'm proclaiming the truth so that when Judgment Day comes, they won't have any excuse... and every one of them is going to be cast headfirst into the lake of fire!"

Yikes! Considering how many ugly things like this that have been spoken in the name of Christianity, is it any wonder so many have negative perceptions of those who "share their faith" openly? It's easy to understand why people reacted negatively to Stan's message of wrath and judgment, but how can you help them get beyond the negativity to embrace the generous Jesus you're coming to know?

Stop Fearing the Culture

An essential first step is to overcome your fear of the culture. In the past couple of decades many popular preachers and prominent religious organizations have spent millions fanning the flames of this fear. Among other things, they cautioned Christians to beware of the hidden subliminal messages in modern music and movies; they explained how exposure to secular humanism and the homosexual agenda subtly erodes traditional moral values; they warned that watching *The Simpsons* on TV or reading the Harry Potter books could turn innocent kids into delinquents or even Satanists. They told us to be afraid. Be very afraid—nearly everything in the culture around you is a life-threatening menace to your Christian faith!

The basic message that comes across is that you should be scared to death of everyone and everything that doesn't pass the most stringent moral and spiritual tests. Again we say "Yuck!" Embracing this separatist subculture of perpetual anxiety not only shrinks your soul, it severely limits your circle of friends. Worst of all, it leads to a defensive isolation that's the polar opposite of the overflowing generosity of Jesus.

Our natural response to fear is either fight or flight. People who fear the culture usually adopt one of these two responses: They either try to attack it or run away from it. The "attackers" have been some of the prime movers of what in the late 1980s and early 1990s became known as the "culture wars." They drew political battle lines around hot-button issues such as abortion, pornography, and homosexuality, and then began waging heated legislative and public relations wars.

And it is important to stand up for what we believe is right, but political passions can all too easily eclipse the love of Jesus until we become guilty of hating the very people Jesus died for. We're reminded of what Jesus taught in Matthew 7:1-5. Since we're sinners ourselves, attacking sin *in someone else's life* is very tricky business:

> "Do not judge others, and you will not be judged. For you will be treated as you treat others. The standard you use in judging is the standard by which you will be judged.

> "And why worry about a speck in your friend's eye when you have a log in your own? How can you think of saying to your friend, 'Let me help you get rid of that speck in your eye,' when you can't see past the log in your own eye? Hypocrite! First get rid of the log in your own eye; then you will see well enough to deal with the speck in your friend's eye."

To have any chance of sharing the generous love of Jesus, we've got to remove the "log" of self-righteousness from our own lives and stop attaching our own conditions to God's free gift of love. Remember what Romans 5:8 teaches: There is nothing superior about you—or any follower of Christ, for that matter— compared to the "worst" sinner you can think of. "But God demonstrates his own love for us in this: While we were still sinners, Christ died for us" (NIV). If we're to imitate our Lord, we too must accept folks actively involved in sinful actions and lifestyles precisely as he accepts us— unconditionally.

We're not called to judge the people of the world. We're called to love them.

We've talked about this before, but one reason so many Christians have a hard time with this teaching is that they confuse acceptance with approval. When Jesus died for our sins he wasn't *endorsing* them, he was offering himself as the one and only cure for their soul-killing effects. If Jesus can do this for us, can't we accept our fellow sinners without having to endorse the bad things they do? We don't know about you, but there are very few people—even the ones we love the most—whose every action we can approve of without reservation. We'll say it again: *Acceptance is not approval!*

Some members of evangelical churches in California have decided to boldly put this principle into action by reaching out in love to participants in the annual Gay/Lesbian Pride Festival held in their city. Given the in-your-face activism of many of the marchers, usually if churches respond at all it's to protest the parade. But this group decided to focus on God's love for the participants instead. They gave away "God Loves You" stickers along with several hundred multicolored lilies. They also painted faces, decorated the arms of marchers, took free pictures, and had all kinds of wonderful conversations with the attendees. On a table with a small sign on it, they placed free Bibles and *God's Promises for Your Every Need* booklets—every one of which was taken by a marcher. John, one of the leaders of this audacious outreach, explains what happened:

> Our booth was opposite the main stage and strategically placed between the Los Angeles Police Department recruiting booth (containing officers in full gear and a squad car) and the gay and lesbian anti-violence booth. With hundreds of flowers and balloons decorating our booth we stood out visually from the very start.
>
> God gave us lots of wonderful appointments with people. Face painting, handing out flowers, and taking Polaroid pictures out in front of our booth provided great openings for longer connections with people. Our team was thrilled and blessed by the interactions.
>
> Gays and lesbians are often turned off by the "hate the sin, love the sinner" slogan Christians use on them. They hear "*hate the sin*," loud

and clear, but they hardly ever witness the *love* part lived out in practical ways. As a result, when we say, "But we love you," after denouncing their sin, they interpret us to mean: "We love you as long as you stay out of our city and as far from us as possible...so we won't have to deal with you."

In contrast, the sticker we gave away said, "God Loves You." *Period.* We stuck with that theme, pointing every lost person we met to the Good Shepherd—and relying on Jesus to take care of the rest. A number of the people that we talked with asked, "Can *anyone* come to your church?"

The answer, of course, was "yes," (some almost cried when they heard this) and we gladly gave them our address.

If this story makes you uncomfortable, that's probably a good thing. It directly confronts us with how we treat folks many would rather avoid. This avoidance is the second natural response to fear of the culture—it's the flight tendency. Simply put, it's very tempting to avoid those we don't know how to deal with. Of course, once again, that's not what Jesus taught. In Matthew 25:35-40 he said that when we feed the hungry, or welcome strangers and outcasts into our homes, or clothe the naked, or look after the sick, or visit forgotten prisoners, it is exactly as if we are doing it *for him*. The people Jesus is talking about are the ones members of polite society usually prefer to avoid—those who live at the margins of our culture both economically and morally. While some are ostracized for their lifestyle choices, others are addicts and even criminals. And many of them aren't necessarily who your mother might consider *nice, virtuous* people.

Still, Jesus says when we show compassion to these outsiders, we're actually showing love for him. Maybe we should get rid of those bracelets that say "WWJD" (What Would Jesus Do?) and replace them with new ones that say "HATJ" (How Am I Treating Jesus?). Are we walking by on the other side of the road—doing everything we can to avoid the hurting people around us—or are we stopping, kneeling down, and doing what we can to love and serve them?

Steve's wife, Janie, pushed what many people might see as the limits of Jesus' teaching in Matthew 25 when she decided to reach out to an infamous pornographer who had opened up an "adult" superstore in Cincinnati. *Hustler* magazine publisher, Larry Flint and his brother Jimmy, had unflinchingly watched protestors intimidate their store's clients by taking customers' photos or writing down their license plate numbers—but what Janie did shocked them in a much more intriguing way. Janie walked up to Jimmy Flint in the downtown Hustler store and asked if he would let her and her outreach team clean the store's restrooms for free.

"Why would you want to do that?" Jimmy asked.

As usual Janie said, "It's just our way of saying God loves you."

Jimmy scratched his head in confusion and remarked, "I thought all you people hated us."

Janie smiled and said, "No, we don't hate you at all...we *really* love you and we *really* want to clean your toilets."

Totally disarmed and more than slightly amused, Jimmy showed the teams to the restrooms and watched them go to work. He was so impressed he commented on their thoroughness, and asked the group several questions about their church. When they were done, he enthusiastically thanked them saying, "I like you guys. You're welcome here any time!"

Weeks later, Steve encountered Jimmy sitting in a seat near him on an airplane. Steve picked up the conversation where Janie and her team had left it. Jimmy was full of questions about the kind of people who put loving and serving ahead of attacking and condemning. Jimmy felt accepted, and even though Steve and Janie have never approved or endorsed the business he was in, they became friends.

Years later, when Steve nearly died from a freak medical accident, the first person to call and check on his condition was Jimmy Flint.

Little acts of kindness and acceptance had made a lasting impression on Jimmy and made him want to respond in kind.

Loving is far better than fighting or fleeing because loving the people as "Jesus in disguise" will transform both you and them. And doing so will allow your sharing to become more love-based and less fear-based. So when you speak up about *God's* love, people will see your love for them and not your fear of them. Allowing *God's* love for people to overwhelm *your* fear of them is the true secret of sharing. *The Message* version of 1 John 4:18 says, "There is no room in love for fear. Well-formed love banishes fear. Since fear is crippling, a fearful life—fear of death, fear of judgment—is one not yet fully formed in love." The key, though, to all of this is to remember the fountain: God is your source of water. The reason many churches and religious leaders fear culture is because many—even "good" Christians—have succumbed to it...some even during their efforts to reach people in the world. In order to overflow to the world—in order to live in the world, but not be of the world—you have to be filled up with God's love. It *is* a dangerous world out there—one where the Thief is very present— so you need to be filled up with God's love and strength as you endeavor to share his love with everyone.

Our last reading is about a life that's fully formed in love—one that creates and transmits a legacy of love that will bear fruit long after you've left this planet.

getting your **feet wet**

Think of a place that you can go where it's likely that you'll come into contact with people who have different values and beliefs than you do. It might be a concert, a community event, a coffee shop, or a nightclub. Before you go, pray that God would fill you with his strength and love as you engage with people. Once there, look around you and imagine the face of Jesus superimposed over the faces of the people you see.

If opportunity arises, strike up a conversation with one of the people there and listen carefully and nonjudgmentally to find out what's on that person's mind. If the person asks what's on your mind, share what you're honestly thinking. Let God direct the conversation and watch what happens.

the **reflection** *pool*

>> When you think of evangelism, or sharing God's love with others, what frightens you? How might loving people help you overcome that fear?

>> Do you fight, flee, or express love to the culture—or a mix of all three? Why?

>> What's a practical way you can personally show God's love to someone whose lifestyle you don't agree with?

"Then the glory of the Lord will be revealed, and all people will see it together.

The Lord has spoken."

—ISAIAH 40:5

"Oh the folly of any mind that would explain God before obeying him! That would map out the character of God instead of crying, Lord what wouldst thou have me do?"

—George MacDonald

READING 25

a lifetime of serving your world

Imagine you're at the end of your life. You've done everything you dreamed of doing. You've had a long and fruitful life of walking with God. The record of your experiences is full of meaning—bursting with love and great accomplishments. Everything you wanted has happened...*except for one thing.*

That's the story of Simeon, a Jerusalem man we read about in Luke 2:25-33. Simeon was nearing the end of his life, but he was just waiting for one more thing—to see the coming of the Messiah!

Simeon was so closely in tune with God, that Simeon knew he wasn't destined to die until he saw "the Christ" who was coming from God...and would set God's people free. Though Simeon may have been growing deaf in his physical ears, after a lifetime of listening to God, he excelled at hearing God's prompting. Simeon had cultivated this ability—along with the habit of acting on whatever that still, small voice told him to do. This time, God told

Simeon to come to the temple courts on a certain day. So he did...and he was just in time to meet Joseph and Mary as they were bringing the baby Jesus to be circumcised. A life well-lived and a heart open to doing God's will had brought Simeon to the perfect place, and the perfect time, to experience his last and greatest dream come true.

Though Simeon's physical eyes may have been failing, the sharp, well-practiced eyes of his heart beheld what Isaiah 40:5 had proclaimed—the glory of the Lord revealed before him! In exaltation, Simeon softly lifted the tiny Savior of the world in his gnarled old hands saying: "God, you can now release your servant...With my own eyes I've seen your salvation; it's now out in the open for everyone to see" (LUKE 2:29-31, *The Message*). At just that moment, an 84-year-old woman named Anna, who also listened to God, showed up and began loudly singing praise songs and telling anyone who would listen that the baby Simeon held was the Messiah.

This old man and old woman had done it all and seen it all. They'd fully experienced life with all its joy and losses. They'd lived in silent hope and joyful service. They'd lived long enough and deeply enough to see their dreams come true—and to recognize those dreams when they saw them. And now at last, they were ready for God to take them home.

There has been a great deal written and said about discovering your purpose in life, but we could learn a few things from Anna and Simeon. They clearly understood what the Apostle Paul later talked about when he compared living out his purpose to finishing well in the long-distance race of life. Here's how *the Message* version of 2 Timothy 4:7-8 translates what Paul said: "I've run hard right to the finish, believed all the way. All that's left now is the shouting—God's applause!"

Isn't that a great picture? God cheering you on as you come in for the last lap. A life well-lived; a race well-run.

Unfortunately, lots of people out there are running in circles and getting nowhere fast.

But Jesus is inviting you to follow him in leading a life that goes somewhere truly amazing. If you match his pace, and follow him closely, you'll see dreams come true and experience what it means to overflow with life. On the way, you'll touch and inspire many others who will join you on the track to greater joy, deeper peace, and eternal, inexhaustible life.

Don't make the mistake of thinking Christ only makes one invitation and that once you accept his gift of eternal life, you're done. The truth is Jesus is constantly inviting you to proceed higher up and deeper in with him.

Miraculous Timing

Miracles are often a matter of timing—either a natural process being sped up, or just the right string of "amazing coincidences." Part of what makes the story of Simeon and Anna miraculous is that they showed up in exactly the right location, at precisely the right moment, to see their personal prayers answered and their lifetime dreams come true. God delights in answering prayer and performing miracles—even though we often don't recognize them in the moment they're taking place. That's how one of the greatest miracles in Steve's life happened.

From the earliest days of my childhood, I remember being very connected to my dad. Then came the summer of 1968. The Vietnam conflict was at a fever pitch and two of my cousins were killed in action over there. If that wasn't sad enough, in early July my dad came down with a terrible case of pneumonia he couldn't shake. On his birthday, July 10th, the doctors discovered his pneumonia was really lung cancer that had spread throughout his entire body.

To make a long story tragically short, my dad died precisely five weeks to the day after he was diagnosed, and five weeks after he turned 39. My 12-year-old life shattered in more pieces than I could count. The time leading up to my dad's death was the most devastating thing I had ever gone through.

My dad had always been a clear-headed, hard-charging guy who led a good life morally and ethically. From the age of 25 to his death he'd been a family man working his way up the corporate ladder to become president of a 400-employee company. The only thing that wasn't clear-cut for him was his spiritual life.

At the time I knew next to nothing about God, but in the days leading up to my father's death, I prayed what I discovered later was a miraculously life-changing prayer. I cried and pleaded with God saying, "Whoever you are, *please save my dad.*"

Unbeknownst to me an hour away, just west of Wichita, God was answering my prayer. My dad's cousin—who'd just had a profound spiritual awakening and invited Jesus into his life about a month before—sensed God telling him to go and share Jesus' love with my dad before he died.

To fully appreciate this story, it's important to realize that my dad had a steady flow of visitors in the hospital each day, and especially on the weekends. This particular Saturday, about four weeks after his diagnosis, he was going downhill fast. His cousin felt God's clear invitation urging him, "Get up now! Go immediately to the hospital, and I'll give you an opportunity to share your story in a way that will get through."

He thought, *"This can't be right. It's Saturday and these are prime visiting hours. His room will be filled with people. I'll never get to speak with him in private."* Still, my dad's cousin felt a continuing sense of urgency. The good news is that he answered God's invitation and in doing so became an answer to my prayer (even though I didn't fully understand exactly how until many years later).

Now I'm unspeakably grateful he took that risk and made that long drive to the hospital. And coincidentally (or miraculously—depending on how you look at it), he got over 90 minutes of uninterrupted time with my dad to tell his story and invite my dad to join him in walking with God. As sick as he was, my dad agreed without hesitation. He prayed a profound and openhearted prayer and asked Jesus *to save him.*

Sadly, the very next day, the cancer advanced to the point that it affected his brain and he was unable to think or communicate clearly. During the last week of his life, he was either in a stupor due to the cancer or due to the massive amounts of morphine he was being given. The timing of his conversation with my cousin had turned out to be just right.

I didn't get this story from my dad's cousin until years later, but for some reason I was very peaceful in the minutes and hours after getting the news my dad had died. I was relieved that his suffering was over, but more than that, I felt a kind of calming presence around me. I know this sounds a little odd, but as I opened the screen door leading into our house that night, I "heard" an inner voice speaking to me.

A still and small voice (I would later learn to recognize) was speaking comfort directly to my 12-year-old spirit.

"From now on" the voice said, *"I'll be your Father."* Years later I discovered Psalm 68:5 and underlined the part that explains that God is a "father to the fatherless."

Steve's dad's cousin was so filled up with God that he heard the Holy Spirit's voice calling him to get in his car and go share his story. As he obeyed, God's love flowed out from him and into Steve's father in exactly the right moment that Steve's dad was ready to receive it. Those actions not only helped answer Steve's prayers but the prayers of many others who loved Steve's dad.

God answers prayers even when you're not aware of his loving presence in your life. God is constantly inviting you to get to know him better, to follow him more closely, and to act on loving, miracle-producing impulses from his Spirit. You may never know of all the prayers you've helped to answer or all the lives you've helped to change as you reach out and allow God's love to flow into you and out into the world around you.

Listen Closely

In this book you've heard scores of stories and read several dozen passages of Scripture about how God wants to fill you up with his love and pour out "streams of living water" into the world of your relationships. If this is something you're longing for and if you want your life to "bear fruit that will last," we have a few final words of advice for you. First, like Simeon, Anna, Steve's dad's cousin, and countless followers of Jesus before you, tune your ear to hear God's voice. God is not just content to speak to you from time to time. As you grow in your ability to perceive God's voice, you'll recognize that he's speaking to you constantly. God is communicating through what's written in the Bible and what the Holy Spirit is saying in your heart. If you're willing to pay attention, God is inviting you to begin writing miraculous stories in your own life and in the lives of your world. Today, if you'll listen closely, God is knocking on the door of your heart. If you'll open up and go with him, God will lead you on adventures so cool and so exciting you won't be able to shut up about them.

There are so many people all around you who need an encouraging word or a practical touch of God's love with no strings attached—it's your world, and God's inviting you to share his love with it.

If you will hone in on God's heart for almost any individual person, you'll get a specific assignment telling you how to proceed. It's not complicated, no matter what you've thought in the past.

Final Words

Your world—the world God wants you to reach with his love, that final tier of your fountain—it's all around you. Take a step out your front door and you'll see it there, stretching out before you. People walking their dogs and getting into their cars. People laughing and talking and drinking coffee. People hurting and crying and starving for food. All of them. They're all longing. They're all within your reach. They're all part of the world God has put you in—the personal sphere of influence God has given you.

Mary and Joseph, the Apostles Peter and Paul, St. Francis, Martin Luther, Bill Bright, Mother Teresa, Billy Graham, Brother Andrew. Ordinary people who constantly received God's love and poured it out on the world around them. Go ahead and add your name to the list—your world will never be the same.

And when the day finally comes that you're approaching the end of a life of walking with God—when you're looking back through the catalog of lives you've touched and helped to transform with Christ's love—it's our prayer that all of God's dreams for your life will have come true...*and that you will taste heaven's joys long before you arrive there.*

getting your **feet wet**

Picture yourself on your deathbed after a long and fruitful life. Friends and family have come to say goodbye, to celebrate your greatest accomplishments, and to tell stories about the lives you've touched.

Who would you want to be there and what would you like them to be talking about?

the **reflection** *pool*

>> It's a morbid question, sure, but a good one—what would you want written on your headstone? In other words, what do you want to be known for?

>> How can you begin building that legacy now?

>> How have the concepts of *Outflow* challenged the way you view your life as a Christian? How will that affect the way you live your life from here on out?

the deep end

MINUTE-BY-MINUTE MISSIONS

Sharing Jesus' love with your world isn't only about going on a mission trip to a *foreign* country every year—it's not necessarily about foreign missions at all. Instead, it's about intentionally and graciously sharing Jesus' love with everyone in *your* world. It's about overflowing so generously that no one gets left out—there isn't anyone in your life who doesn't get "splashed" by God's love flowing from you.

Use this Deep End experience to intentionally share God's love throughout a day.

By yourself or with your small group, visit a place where lots of people hang out and have fun: an amusement park, a ballgame, the beach...

Before you go, use an old trick to help you remember to share God's love throughout the day: Tie a string around your finger. Use this string as a reminder to smile at people regularly, to make eye contact, to pick up trash, to hold open doors, to ask people's names, to serve people in everyday ways.

You'll also want to set an alarm on your watch or cell phone for the top of every hour. At that time, stop whatever you're doing and get together with your small group or head out on your own to do a "bigger" act of service. Clean a bathroom, hand out water, buy a soda for everyone in line at the concession stand...the ideas are endless!

Being a missionary to your world is about altering your patterns and everyday behavior to serve people, to be aware of people, to share in God's love for people. And it isn't about where you are or what day of the week it is—you could be out having fun at an amusement park, or you could be doing your weekly errands at the grocery store. That's the whole point—it's natural, everyday, overflowing outreach *wherever you are, whatever you're doing*.

And it's all because God first loved you.

group
discussion questions

*Use these questions during your small-group time and dia-
logue together about the fifth week of* Outflow *readings.*

>> Why do you think it's important for each Christian—
individually—to take a personal interest in changing
the world for God?

>> Reading 22 challenges Christians to change their
perspectives by focusing outward instead of inward.
When has focusing outward helped you grow personally and share God's love more effectively? Describe
the situation.

>> How could loving the world become a part of your life-
style and not just something you make yourself do?

>> When you think of evangelism, or sharing God's love
with others, what frightens you? How might loving
people help you overcome that fear?

>> It's a morbid question, sure, but a good one: What
would you want written on your headstone? In other
words, what do you want to be known for? How can
you begin building that legacy now?

>> How have the concepts of *Outflow* challenged the way
you view your life as a Christian? How will that affect
the way you live your life from here on out?

about the authors

STEVE SJOGREN

is the pioneer of the modern outward-focused church movement—something that began over 20 years ago when he planted a small church in Cincinnati. Recognized today as Vineyard Community Church, it has grown from 30 to more than 6,000 weekly attendees and has been responsible for birthing over 22 congregations in the greater Cincinnati area.

Currently, Steve is planting a new church on the east side of Tampa, Florida. CoastlandTampa (.com) will be based on the principles of *Outflow*—and will encourage its members to live a life of generosity and practical love every day.

In addition to this significant and crucial church launch in Florida, Steve heads up ServeCoach.com, a professional coaching group dedicated to helping leaders become "unstuck" when they come to a plateau in their ministry or career. To date, this innovative service has helped over 1,000 leaders.

Steve is the author and co-author of such groundbreaking works as *Conspiracy of Kindness, 101 Ways to Reach Your Community, Irresistible Evangelism,* and *The Day I Died.*

STEVE SJOGREN ONLINE

SERVANTEVANGELISM.COM
{http://www.servantevangelism.com} *Steve Sjogren's portal to all things concerning servant evangelism and the outward focused life.*

SERVE! EZINE
{http://www.serve-others.com} *A monthly ezine on living the outward focused life.*

OUTWARDBUZZ.COM
{http://www.outwardbuzz.com} *A daily video podcast on outward focused living.*

SERVECOACH.COM
{http://www.servecoach.com} *Contacting Steve for leadership and outward focused coaching.*

DAVE PING

brings over 20 years of outreach and training experience to his role as Executive Director of Equipping
Ministries International. Under his leadership, EMI
has taught outward-focused ministry skills to over
100,000 pastors, missionaries, and volunteer leaders
in 55 countries. Dave is a highly practical, creative,
and entertaining conference speaker. He has authored interactive training courses and co-authored such popular books as *Listening for Heaven's
Sake, Irresistible Evangelism,* and *Quick-to-Listen Leaders.*

**The ultimate success (or failure) of your family,
small group, ministry, or congregation depends
on the quality of your relationships.**

Equipping Ministries International, Inc. will help you
release the hidden potential of Christian relationships
through healthy living and outward-focused ministry.
Creating an 'Outflow Culture' puts you and your church in a
place of influence that directly and positively affects church
growth, community empowerment, and world outreach.

Imagine the growth and power you and your church could experience by ingrain-
ing such biblical skills as being quick to listen, speaking the truth in love,
renewing your mind, and practicing irresistible evangelism into your daily lives.
If you want to revolutionize your volunteer, small group, and staff training, while
making a greater impact on your community, EMI is a great place to start.

Proven Biblical Solutions:

EMI's training is practical, interactive, fun, and backed up by over 25 years of
hands-on experience in churches and organizations like yours. Best of all, EMI
training is specially designed to be handed over to ordinary lay people who
can train others for years to come.

Check out Equipping Ministries International's practical training by going to
www.equippingministries.org or calling 1-800-364-4769.